FTCE
Exceptional Student Education K-12

SECRETS

Study Guide
Your Key to Exam Success

FTCE Subject Test Review for the
Florida Teacher
Certification Examinations

Dear Future Exam Success Story:

First of all, **THANK YOU** for purchasing Mometrix study materials!

Second, congratulations! You are one of the few determined test-takers who are committed to doing whatever it takes to excel on your exam. **You have come to the right place.** We developed these study materials with one goal in mind: to deliver you the information you need in a format that's concise and easy to use.

In addition to optimizing your guide for the content of the test, we've outlined our recommended steps for breaking down the preparation process into small, attainable goals so you can make sure you stay on track.

We've also analyzed the entire test-taking process, identifying the most common pitfalls and showing how you can overcome them and be ready for any curveball the test throws you.

Standardized testing is one of the biggest obstacles on your road to success, which only increases the importance of doing well in the high-pressure, high-stakes environment of test day. Your results on this test could have a significant impact on your future, and this guide provides the information and practical advice to help you achieve your full potential on test day.

Your success is our success

We would love to hear from you! If you would like to share the story of your exam success or if you have any questions or comments in regard to our products, please contact us at **800-673-8175** or **support@mometrix.com**.

Thanks again for your business and we wish you continued success!

Sincerely,
The Mometrix Test Preparation Team

Need more help? Check out our flashcards at: http://MometrixFlashcards.com/FTCE

TABLE OF CONTENTS

INTRODUCTION _____ 1

SECRET KEY #1 – PLAN BIG, STUDY SMALL _____ 2
    INFORMATION ORGANIZATION _____ 2
    TIME MANAGEMENT _____ 2
    STUDY ENVIRONMENT _____ 2

SECRET KEY #2 – MAKE YOUR STUDYING COUNT _____ 3
    RETENTION _____ 3
    MODALITY _____ 3

SECRET KEY #3 – PRACTICE THE RIGHT WAY _____ 4
    PRACTICE TEST STRATEGY _____ 5

SECRET KEY #4 – PACE YOURSELF _____ 6

SECRET KEY #5 – HAVE A PLAN FOR GUESSING _____ 7
    WHEN TO START THE GUESSING PROCESS _____ 7
    HOW TO NARROW DOWN THE CHOICES _____ 8
    WHICH ANSWER TO CHOOSE _____ 9

TEST-TAKING STRATEGIES _____ 10
    QUESTION STRATEGIES _____ 10
    ANSWER CHOICE STRATEGIES _____ 11
    GENERAL STRATEGIES _____ 12
    FINAL NOTES _____ 13

FOUNDATIONS OF EXCEPTIONAL STUDENT EDUCATION _____ 15

ASSESSMENT AND EVALUATION _____ 43

INSTRUCTIONAL PRACTICES IN EXCEPTIONAL STUDENT EDUCATION _____ 61

POSITIVE BEHAVIORAL SUPPORT PROCESS _____ 69

MULTIPLE LITERACIES AND COMMUNICATION SKILLS _____ 74

TRANSITION PROCESS _____ 86

FTCE PRACTICE TEST _____ 98

ANSWER KEY AND EXPLANATIONS _____ 113

HOW TO OVERCOME TEST ANXIETY _____ 130
    CAUSES OF TEST ANXIETY _____ 130
    ELEMENTS OF TEST ANXIETY _____ 131
    EFFECTS OF TEST ANXIETY _____ 131
    PHYSICAL STEPS FOR BEATING TEST ANXIETY _____ 132
    MENTAL STEPS FOR BEATING TEST ANXIETY _____ 133
    STUDY STRATEGY _____ 134
    TEST TIPS _____ 136
    IMPORTANT QUALIFICATION _____ 137

THANK YOU _____ 138

Introduction

Thank you for purchasing this resource! You have made the choice to prepare yourself for a test that could have a huge impact on your future, and this guide is designed to help you be fully ready for test day. Obviously, it's important to have a solid understanding of the test material, but you also need to be prepared for the unique environment and stressors of the test, so that you can perform to the best of your abilities.

For this purpose, the first section that appears in this guide is the **Secret Keys**. We've devoted countless hours to meticulously researching what works and what doesn't, and we've boiled down our findings to the five most impactful steps you can take to improve your performance on the test. We start at the beginning with study planning and move through the preparation process, all the way to the testing strategies that will help you get the most out of what you know when you're finally sitting in front of the test.

We recommend that you start preparing for your test as far in advance as possible. However, if you've bought this guide as a last-minute study resource and only have a few days before your test, we recommend that you skip over the first two Secret Keys since they address a long-term study plan.

If you struggle with **test anxiety**, we strongly encourage you to check out our recommendations for how you can overcome it. Test anxiety is a formidable foe, but it can be beaten, and we want to make sure you have the tools you need to defeat it.

Secret Key #1 – Plan Big, Study Small

There's a lot riding on your performance. If you want to ace this test, you're going to need to keep your skills sharp and the material fresh in your mind. You need a plan that lets you review everything you need to know while still fitting in your schedule. We'll break this strategy down into three categories.

Information Organization

Start with the information you already have: the official test outline. From this, you can make a complete list of all the concepts you need to cover before the test. Organize these concepts into groups that can be studied together, and create a list of any related vocabulary you need to learn so you can brush up on any difficult terms. You'll want to keep this vocabulary list handy once you actually start studying since you may need to add to it along the way.

Time Management

Once you have your set of study concepts, decide how to spread them out over the time you have left before the test. Break your study plan into small, clear goals so you have a manageable task for each day and know exactly what you're doing. Then just focus on one small step at a time. When you manage your time this way, you don't need to spend hours at a time studying. Studying a small block of content for a short period each day helps you retain information better and avoid stressing over how much you have left to do. You can relax knowing that you have a plan to cover everything in time. In order for this strategy to be effective though, you have to start studying early and stick to your schedule. Avoid the exhaustion and futility that comes from last-minute cramming!

Study Environment

The environment you study in has a big impact on your learning. Studying in a coffee shop, while probably more enjoyable, is not likely to be as fruitful as studying in a quiet room. It's important to keep distractions to a minimum. You're only planning to study for a short block of time, so make the most of it. Don't pause to check your phone or get up to find a snack. It's also important to **avoid multitasking**. Research has consistently shown that multitasking will make your studying dramatically less effective. Your study area should also be comfortable and well-lit so you don't have the distraction of straining your eyes or sitting on an uncomfortable chair.

The time of day you study is also important. You want to be rested and alert. Don't wait until just before bedtime. Study when you'll be most likely to comprehend and remember. Even better, if you know what time of day your test will be, set that time aside for study. That way your brain will be used to working on that subject at that specific time and you'll have a better chance of recalling information.

Finally, it can be helpful to team up with others who are studying for the same test. Your actual studying should be done in as isolated an environment as possible, but the work of organizing the information and setting up the study plan can be divided up. In between study sessions, you can discuss with your teammates the concepts that you're all studying and quiz each other on the details. Just be sure that your teammates are as serious about the test as you are. If you find that your study time is being replaced with social time, you might need to find a new team.

Secret Key #2 – Make Your Studying Count

You're devoting a lot of time and effort to preparing for this test, so you want to be absolutely certain it will pay off. This means doing more than just reading the content and hoping you can remember it on test day. It's important to make every minute of study count. There are two main areas you can focus on to make your studying count:

Retention

It doesn't matter how much time you study if you can't remember the material. You need to make sure you are retaining the concepts. To check your retention of the information you're learning, try recalling it at later times with minimal prompting. Try carrying around flashcards and glance at one or two from time to time or ask a friend who's also studying for the test to quiz you.

To enhance your retention, look for ways to put the information into practice so that you can apply it rather than simply recalling it. If you're using the information in practical ways, it will be much easier to remember. Similarly, it helps to solidify a concept in your mind if you're not only reading it to yourself but also explaining it to someone else. Ask a friend to let you teach them about a concept you're a little shaky on (or speak aloud to an imaginary audience if necessary). As you try to summarize, define, give examples, and answer your friend's questions, you'll understand the concepts better and they will stay with you longer. Finally, step back for a big picture view and ask yourself how each piece of information fits with the whole subject. When you link the different concepts together and see them working together as a whole, it's easier to remember the individual components.

Finally, practice showing your work on any multi-step problems, even if you're just studying. Writing out each step you take to solve a problem will help solidify the process in your mind, and you'll be more likely to remember it during the test.

Modality

Modality simply refers to the means or method by which you study. Choosing a study modality that fits your own individual learning style is crucial. No two people learn best in exactly the same way, so it's important to know your strengths and use them to your advantage.

For example, if you learn best by visualization, focus on visualizing a concept in your mind and draw an image or a diagram. Try color-coding your notes, illustrating them, or creating symbols that will trigger your mind to recall a learned concept. If you learn best by hearing or discussing information, find a study partner who learns the same way or read aloud to yourself. Think about how to put the information in your own words. Imagine that you are giving a lecture on the topic and record yourself so you can listen to it later.

For any learning style, flashcards can be helpful. Organize the information so you can take advantage of spare moments to review. Underline key words or phrases. Use different colors for different categories. Mnemonic devices (such as creating a short list in which every item starts with the same letter) can also help with retention. Find what works best for you and use it to store the information in your mind most effectively and easily.

Secret Key #3 – Practice the Right Way

Your success on test day depends not only on how many hours you put into preparing, but also on whether you prepared the right way. It's good to check along the way to see if your studying is paying off. One of the most effective ways to do this is by taking practice tests to evaluate your progress. Practice tests are useful because they show exactly where you need to improve. Every time you take a practice test, pay special attention to these three groups of questions:

- The questions you got wrong
- The questions you had to guess on, even if you guessed right
- The questions you found difficult or slow to work through

This will show you exactly what your weak areas are, and where you need to devote more study time. Ask yourself why each of these questions gave you trouble. Was it because you didn't understand the material? Was it because you didn't remember the vocabulary? Do you need more repetitions on this type of question to build speed and confidence? Dig into those questions and figure out how you can strengthen your weak areas as you go back to review the material.

Additionally, many practice tests have a section explaining the answer choices. It can be tempting to read the explanation and think that you now have a good understanding of the concept. However, an explanation likely only covers part of the question's broader context. Even if the explanation makes sense, **go back and investigate** every concept related to the question until you're positive you have a thorough understanding.

As you go along, keep in mind that the practice test is just that: practice. Memorizing these questions and answers will not be very helpful on the actual test because it is unlikely to have any of the same exact questions. If you only know the right answers to the sample questions, you won't be prepared for the real thing. **Study the concepts** until you understand them fully, and then you'll be able to answer any question that shows up on the test.

It's important to wait on the practice tests until you're ready. If you take a test on your first day of study, you may be overwhelmed by the amount of material covered and how much you need to learn. Work up to it gradually.

On test day, you'll need to be prepared for answering questions, managing your time, and using the test-taking strategies you've learned. It's a lot to balance, like a mental marathon that will have a big impact on your future. Like training for a marathon, you'll need to start slowly and work your way up. When test day arrives, you'll be ready.

Start with the strategies you've read in the first two Secret Keys—plan your course and study in the way that works best for you. If you have time, consider using multiple study resources to get different approaches to the same concepts. It can be helpful to see difficult concepts from more than one angle. Then find a good source for practice tests. Many times, the test website will suggest potential study resources or provide sample tests.

Practice Test Strategy

If you're able to find at least three practice tests, we recommend this strategy:

Untimed and Open-Book Practice

Take the first test with no time constraints and with your notes and study guide handy. Take your time and focus on applying the strategies you've learned.

Timed and Open-Book Practice

Take the second practice test open-book as well, but set a timer and practice pacing yourself to finish in time.

Timed and Closed-Book Practice

Take any other practice tests as if it were test day. Set a timer and put away your study materials. Sit at a table or desk in a quiet room, imagine yourself at the testing center, and answer questions as quickly and accurately as possible.

Keep repeating timed and closed-book tests on a regular basis until you run out of practice tests or it's time for the actual test. Your mind will be ready for the schedule and stress of test day, and you'll be able to focus on recalling the material you've learned.

Secret Key #4 – Pace Yourself

Once you're fully prepared for the material on the test, your biggest challenge on test day will be managing your time. Just knowing that the clock is ticking can make you panic even if you have plenty of time left. Work on pacing yourself so you can build confidence against the time constraints of the exam. Pacing is a difficult skill to master, especially in a high-pressure environment, so **practice is vital**.

Set time expectations for your pace based on how much time is available. For example, if a section has 60 questions and the time limit is 30 minutes, you know you have to average 30 seconds or less per question in order to answer them all. Although 30 seconds is the hard limit, set 25 seconds per question as your goal, so you reserve extra time to spend on harder questions. When you budget extra time for the harder questions, you no longer have any reason to stress when those questions take longer to answer.

Don't let this time expectation distract you from working through the test at a calm, steady pace, but keep it in mind so you don't spend too much time on any one question. Recognize that taking extra time on one question you don't understand may keep you from answering two that you do understand later in the test. If your time limit for a question is up and you're still not sure of the answer, mark it and move on, and come back to it later if the time and the test format allow. If the testing format doesn't allow you to return to earlier questions, just make an educated guess; then put it out of your mind and move on.

On the easier questions, be careful not to rush. It may seem wise to hurry through them so you have more time for the challenging ones, but it's not worth missing one if you know the concept and just didn't take the time to read the question fully. Work efficiently but make sure you understand the question and have looked at all of the answer choices, since more than one may seem right at first.

Even if you're paying attention to the time, you may find yourself a little behind at some point. You should speed up to get back on track, but do so wisely. Don't panic; just take a few seconds less on each question until you're caught up. Don't guess without thinking, but do look through the answer choices and eliminate any you know are wrong. If you can get down to two choices, it is often worthwhile to guess from those. Once you've chosen an answer, move on and don't dwell on any that you skipped or had to hurry through. If a question was taking too long, chances are it was one of the harder ones, so you weren't as likely to get it right anyway.

On the other hand, if you find yourself getting ahead of schedule, it may be beneficial to slow down a little. The more quickly you work, the more likely you are to make a careless mistake that will affect your score. You've budgeted time for each question, so don't be afraid to spend that time. Practice an efficient but careful pace to get the most out of the time you have.

Secret Key #5 – Have a Plan for Guessing

When you're taking the test, you may find yourself stuck on a question. Some of the answer choices seem better than others, but you don't see the one answer choice that is obviously correct. What do you do?

The scenario described above is very common, yet most test takers have not effectively prepared for it. Developing and practicing a plan for guessing may be one of the single most effective uses of your time as you get ready for the exam.

In developing your plan for guessing, there are three questions to address:

- When should you start the guessing process?
- How should you narrow down the choices?
- Which answer should you choose?

When to Start the Guessing Process

Unless your plan for guessing is to select C every time (which, despite its merits, is not what we recommend), you need to leave yourself enough time to apply your answer elimination strategies. Since you have a limited amount of time for each question, that means that if you're going to give yourself the best shot at guessing correctly, you have to decide quickly whether or not you will guess.

Of course, the best-case scenario is that you don't have to guess at all, so first, see if you can answer the question based on your knowledge of the subject and basic reasoning skills. Focus on the key words in the question and try to jog your memory of related topics. Give yourself a chance to bring the knowledge to mind, but once you realize that you don't have (or you can't access) the knowledge you need to answer the question, it's time to start the guessing process.

It's almost always better to start the guessing process too early than too late. It only takes a few seconds to remember something and answer the question from knowledge. Carefully eliminating wrong answer choices takes longer. Plus, going through the process of eliminating answer choices can actually help jog your memory.

Summary: Start the guessing process as soon as you decide that you can't answer the question based on your knowledge.

How to Narrow Down the Choices

The next chapter in this book (**Test-Taking Strategies**) includes a wide range of strategies for how to approach questions and how to look for answer choices to eliminate. You will definitely want to read those carefully, practice them, and figure out which ones work best for you. Here though, we're going to address a mindset rather than a particular strategy.

Your chances of guessing an answer correctly depend on how many options you are choosing from.

How many choices you have	How likely you are to guess correctly
5	20%
4	25%
3	33%
2	50%
1	100%

You can see from this chart just how valuable it is to be able to eliminate incorrect answers and make an educated guess, but there are two things that many test takers do that cause them to miss out on the benefits of guessing:

- Accidentally eliminating the correct answer
- Selecting an answer based on an impression

We'll look at the first one here, and the second one in the next section.

To avoid accidentally eliminating the correct answer, we recommend a thought exercise called **the $5 challenge**. In this challenge, you only eliminate an answer choice from contention if you are willing to bet $5 on it being wrong. Why $5? Five dollars is a small but not insignificant amount of money. It's an amount you could afford to lose but wouldn't want to throw away. And while losing $5 once might not hurt too much, doing it twenty times will set you back $100. In the same way, each small decision you make—eliminating a choice here, guessing on a question there—won't by itself impact your score very much, but when you put them all together, they can make a big difference. By holding each answer choice elimination decision to a higher standard, you can reduce the risk of accidentally eliminating the correct answer.

The $5 challenge can also be applied in a positive sense: If you are willing to bet $5 that an answer choice *is* correct, go ahead and mark it as correct.

Summary: Only eliminate an answer choice if you are willing to bet $5 that it is wrong.

Which Answer to Choose

You're taking the test. You've run into a hard question and decided you'll have to guess. You've eliminated all the answer choices you're willing to bet $5 on. Now you have to pick an answer. Why do we even need to talk about this? Why can't you just pick whichever one you feel like when the time comes?

The answer to these questions is that if you don't come into the test with a plan, you'll rely on your impression to select an answer choice, and if you do that, you risk falling into a trap. The test writers know that everyone who takes their test will be guessing on some of the questions, so they intentionally write wrong answer choices to seem plausible. You still have to pick an answer though, and if the wrong answer choices are designed to look right, how can you ever be sure that you're not falling for their trap? The best solution we've found to this dilemma is to take the decision out of your hands entirely. Here is the process we recommend:

Once you've eliminated any choices that you are confident (willing to bet $5) are wrong, select the first remaining choice as your answer.

Whether you choose to select the first remaining choice, the second, or the last, the important thing is that you use some preselected standard. Using this approach guarantees that you will not be enticed into selecting an answer choice that looks right, because you are not basing your decision on how the answer choices look.

This is not meant to make you question your knowledge. Instead, it is to help you recognize the difference between your knowledge and your impressions. There's a huge difference between thinking an answer is right because of what you know, and thinking an answer is right because it looks or sounds like it should be right.

Summary: To ensure that your selection is appropriately random, make a predetermined selection from among all answer choices you have not eliminated.

Test-Taking Strategies

This section contains a list of test-taking strategies that you may find helpful as you work through the test. By taking what you know and applying logical thought, you can maximize your chances of answering any question correctly!

It is very important to realize that every question is different and every person is different: no single strategy will work on every question, and no single strategy will work for every person. That's why we've included all of them here, so you can try them out and determine which ones work best for different types of questions and which ones work best for you.

Question Strategies

Read Carefully

Read the question and answer choices carefully. Don't miss the question because you misread the terms. You have plenty of time to read each question thoroughly and make sure you understand what is being asked. Yet a happy medium must be attained, so don't waste too much time. You must read carefully, but efficiently.

Contextual Clues

Look for contextual clues. If the question includes a word you are not familiar with, look at the immediate context for some indication of what the word might mean. Contextual clues can often give you all the information you need to decipher the meaning of an unfamiliar word. Even if you can't determine the meaning, you may be able to narrow down the possibilities enough to make a solid guess at the answer to the question.

Prefixes

If you're having trouble with a word in the question or answer choices, try dissecting it. Take advantage of every clue that the word might include. Prefixes and suffixes can be a huge help. Usually they allow you to determine a basic meaning. Pre- means before, post- means after, pro - is positive, de- is negative. From prefixes and suffixes, you can get an idea of the general meaning of the word and try to put it into context.

Hedge Words

Watch out for critical hedge words, such as *likely, may, can, sometimes, often, almost, mostly, usually, generally, rarely,* and *sometimes.* Question writers insert these hedge phrases to cover every possibility. Often an answer choice will be wrong simply because it leaves no room for exception. Be on guard for answer choices that have definitive words such as *exactly* and *always.*

Switchback Words

Stay alert for *switchbacks.* These are the words and phrases frequently used to alert you to shifts in thought. The most common switchback words are *but, although,* and *however.* Others include *nevertheless, on the other hand, even though, while, in spite of, despite, regardless of.* Switchback words are important to catch because they can change the direction of the question or an answer choice.

Face Value

When in doubt, use common sense. Accept the situation in the problem at face value. Don't read too much into it. These problems will not require you to make wild assumptions. If you have to go beyond creativity and warp time or space in order to have an answer choice fit the question, then you should move on and consider the other answer choices. These are normal problems rooted in reality. The applicable relationship or explanation may not be readily apparent, but it is there for you to figure out. Use your common sense to interpret anything that isn't clear.

Answer Choice Strategies

Answer Selection

The most thorough way to pick an answer choice is to identify and eliminate wrong answers until only one is left, then confirm it is the correct answer. Sometimes an answer choice may immediately seem right, but be careful. The test writers will usually put more than one reasonable answer choice on each question, so take a second to read all of them and make sure that the other choices are not equally obvious. As long as you have time left, it is better to read every answer choice than to pick the first one that looks right without checking the others.

Answer Choice Families

An answer choice family consists of two (in rare cases, three) answer choices that are very similar in construction and cannot all be true at the same time. If you see two answer choices that are direct opposites or parallels, one of them is usually the correct answer. For instance, if one answer choice says that quantity x increases and another either says that quantity x decreases (opposite) or says that quantity y increases (parallel), then those answer choices would fall into the same family. An answer choice that doesn't match the construction of the answer choice family is more likely to be incorrect. Most questions will not have answer choice families, but when they do appear, you should be prepared to recognize them.

Eliminate Answers

Eliminate answer choices as soon as you realize they are wrong, but make sure you consider all possibilities. If you are eliminating answer choices and realize that the last one you are left with is also wrong, don't panic. Start over and consider each choice again. There may be something you missed the first time that you will realize on the second pass.

Avoid Fact Traps

Don't be distracted by an answer choice that is factually true but doesn't answer the question. You are looking for the choice that answers the question. Stay focused on what the question is asking for so you don't accidentally pick an answer that is true but incorrect. Always go back to the question and make sure the answer choice you've selected actually answers the question and is not merely a true statement.

Extreme Statements

In general, you should avoid answers that put forth extreme actions as standard practice or proclaim controversial ideas as established fact. An answer choice that states the "process should be used in certain situations, if..." is much more likely to be correct than one that states the "process should be discontinued completely." The first is a calm rational statement and doesn't even make a definitive, uncompromising stance, using a hedge word *if* to provide wiggle room, whereas the second choice is a radical idea and far more extreme.

Benchmark

As you read through the answer choices and you come across one that seems to answer the question well, mentally select that answer choice. This is not your final answer, but it's the one that will help you evaluate the other answer choices. The one that you selected is your benchmark or standard for judging each of the other answer choices. Every other answer choice must be compared to your benchmark. That choice is correct until proven otherwise by another answer choice beating it. If you find a better answer, then that one becomes your new benchmark. Once you've decided that no other choice answers the question as well as your benchmark, you have your final answer.

Predict the Answer

Before you even start looking at the answer choices, it is often best to try to predict the answer. When you come up with the answer on your own, it is easier to avoid distractions and traps because you will know exactly what to look for. The right answer choice is unlikely to be word-for-word what you came up with, but it should be a close match. Even if you are confident that you have the right answer, you should still take the time to read each option before moving on.

General Strategies

Tough Questions

If you are stumped on a problem or it appears too hard or too difficult, don't waste time. Move on! Remember though, if you can quickly check for obviously incorrect answer choices, your chances of guessing correctly are greatly improved. Before you completely give up, at least try to knock out a couple of possible answers. Eliminate what you can and then guess at the remaining answer choices before moving on.

Check Your Work

Since you will probably not know every term listed and the answer to every question, it is important that you get credit for the ones that you do know. Don't miss any questions through careless mistakes. If at all possible, try to take a second to look back over your answer selection and make sure you've selected the correct answer choice and haven't made a costly careless mistake (such as marking an answer choice that you didn't mean to mark). This quick double check should more than pay for itself in caught mistakes for the time it costs.

Pace Yourself

It's easy to be overwhelmed when you're looking at a page full of questions; your mind is confused and full of random thoughts, and the clock is ticking down faster than you would like. Calm down and maintain the pace that you have set for yourself. Especially as you get down to the last few minutes of the test, don't let the small numbers on the clock make you panic. As long as you are on track by monitoring your pace, you are guaranteed to have time for each question.

Don't Rush

It is very easy to make errors when you are in a hurry. Maintaining a fast pace in answering questions is pointless if it makes you miss questions that you would have gotten right otherwise. Test writers like to include distracting information and wrong answers that seem right. Taking a little extra time to avoid careless mistakes can make all the difference in your test score. Find a pace that allows you to be confident in the answers that you select.

Keep Moving

Panicking will not help you pass the test, so do your best to stay calm and keep moving. Taking deep breaths and going through the answer elimination steps you practiced can help to break through a stress barrier and keep your pace.

Final Notes

The combination of a solid foundation of content knowledge and the confidence that comes from practicing your plan for applying that knowledge is the key to maximizing your performance on test day. As your foundation of content knowledge is built up and strengthened, you'll find that the strategies included in this chapter become more and more effective in helping you quickly sift through the distractions and traps of the test to isolate the correct answer.

Now it's time to move on to the test content chapters of this book, but be sure to keep your goal in mind. As you read, think about how you will be able to apply this information on the test. If you've already seen sample questions for the test and you have an idea of the question format and style, try to come up with questions of your own that you can answer based on what you're reading. This will give you valuable practice applying your knowledge in the same ways you can expect to on test day.

Good luck and good studying!

Foundations of Exceptional Student Education

Individuals with Disabilities Education Act

The Individuals with Disabilities Education Act (**IDEA**) includes six major principles that focus on students' rights and the responsibilities public schools have for educating children with **disabilities**. One of the main principles of the IDEA law is to provide a **free and appropriate public education (FAPE)** suited to the individual needs of a child with a disability. This requires schools to provide special education and related services to students identified as having disabilities. Another purpose of IDEA is to require schools to provide an appropriate **evaluation** of a child with a suspected disability and an **Individualized Education Program (IEP)** for a child with a disability who qualifies under IDEA. Students with IEPs are guaranteed **least restrictive environment (LRE)**, or a guarantee that they are educated in the general education classroom as much as possible. IDEA also ensures **parent participation**, providing a role for parents as equal participants and decision makers. Lastly, **procedural safeguards** also serve to protect parents' rights to advocate for their children with disabilities.

People Protected by Parts B and C of IDEA Law

Early intervention services are provided to children with special needs from birth to age three under **IDEA Part C**. Children from birth to age 3 who are identified as having disabilities and qualify under IDEA receive **Individualized Family Service Plans (IFSPs)**.

Special education and related services are provided to children with disabilities from ages 3 to 21 under **IDEA Part B**. Children ages 3 to 21 who are identified as having disabilities and qualify under IDEA receive educational documents, called **Individualized Education Programs (IEPs)**.

Individualized Education Programs vs. Individualized Family Service Plans

IFSPs and IEPs are both educational documents provided under IDEA to service the rights of children with disabilities and their families. The major differences between IEPs and IFSPs, aside from the ages they service, is that **IFSPs** cover **broader services** for children with disabilities and their families. IFSP services are often provided in the children's homes. **IEPs** focus on special education and related services within the children's **school settings**.

Purpose of IEPs and Function of the PLOPs

An IEP is a written statement for a child with a disability. Its primary purposes are to establish **measurable annual goals** and to list the **services** needed to help the child with a disability meet the annual goals.

The IDEA law mandates that a statement of the child's academic achievement and functional performance be included within the IEP. This statement is called **Present Levels of Performance (PLOPs)**. It provides a snapshot of the student's current performance in school. Present Levels of Performance should also report how a student's disability is affecting, or not affecting, progress in school.

The IDEA law mandates that an **Annual Goals section** be provided within the IEP. Annual goals lay out what a student is expected to learn within a 12-month period. These goals are influenced by the student's PLOPs and are developed using objective, measurable data based on the student's previous academic performance.

Child Find Law

Child Find is part of the Individuals with Disabilities Education Act (IDEA) and states that schools are legally required to find children who have **disabilities** and need **special education** or other services. According to the **Child Find law**, all school districts must have processes for identifying students who need special education and related services. Children with disabilities from birth to age 21, children who are homeschooled, and children in private schools are all covered by the Child Find law. Infants and toddlers can be identified and provided with services so that parents have the right tools in place to meet their children's needs before they enter grade school. The Child Find law does not mean that public schools need to agree to evaluate students when evaluations are requested. Schools may still refuse evaluation if school professionals do not suspect the children of having disabilities.

Steps to Implementing IEPs

The five most important steps in the Individualized Education Program (IEP) process are the identification via "Child Find" or the referral for special education services, evaluation, determination of eligibility, the first IEP meeting at which the IEP is written, and the ongoing provision of services during which progress is measured and reported. The referral can be initiated by a teacher, a special team in the school district, the student's parent, or another professional. The evaluation provides a snapshot of a student's background history, strengths, weaknesses, and academic, behavioral, or social needs. An IEP team of professionals as well as the student's parent(s)/guardian(s) uses the evaluation and any other reports regarding a student's progress to determine if the student is eligible for special education services. Once a student has been found eligible for special education, the first IEP meeting is held during which an IEP is written by a special education teacher or other specialist familiar with the student. The IEP meeting, either initial or annual, is held before the new IEP is implemented. Once the IEP meeting has occurred, services will be provided as detailed in the written IEP, during which the student's progress will continually be measured and reported. The IEP team includes the student, parent(s)/guardian(s), special education teacher, general education teacher, school psychologist, school administrator, appropriate related service professionals, and any other professionals or members that can comment on the student's strengths.

Manifestation Determination

Manifestation determination is a process defined by the Individuals with Disabilities Education Act (IDEA). The **manifestation determination process** is put into effect when a student receiving special education needs to be removed from the educational setting due to a suspension, expulsion or alternative placement. Manifestation determination is the process that determines if the **disciplinary action** resulted from a **manifestation of the student's disability**. This is important because if the action was a manifestation of the disability, the outcome of the disciplinary action may change. During the initial part of this process, relevant data is collected about the student and the circumstances of the offending behavior. The student's Individualized Education Program team determines whether or not the student's behavior was related to the disability. If they determine that the behavior was not related to the disability, the disciplinary action is carried out. If the behavior is determined to be related to the disability, the student is placed back into the original educational setting.

Provision of Title III of the Americans with Disabilities Act

Title III of ADA prohibits the discrimination of people with disabilities in **public accommodations**. Title III seeks to level the playing field of access for people with disabilities participating in public activities. Businesses open to the public, such as schools, restaurants, movie theaters, day care facilities, recreation facilities, doctor's offices, and restaurants, are required to comply with **ADA standards**. Additionally, commercial facilities, such as privately-owned businesses, factories, warehouses, and office buildings, are required to provide access per ADA standards. Title III of ADA outlines the general requirements of the **reasonable modifications** that businesses must provide. Title III also provides detailed, specific requirements for reasonable modifications within businesses and requires new construction and building alterations to abide by ADA regulations. Title III also outlines rules regarding **enforcement of ADA regulations**, such as the consequences for a person or persons participating in discrimination of a person with a disability. Title III provides for **certification of state laws or local building codes**. This means that a state's Assistant Attorney General may issue certification to a place of public accommodation or commercial facility that meets or exceeds the minimum requirements of Title III.

Larry P. v. Riles

The *Larry P. v. Riles* (1977) court case examined possible **cultural discrimination** of African-American students. The court case questioned whether an intelligence quotient (IQ) test was an accurate measurement of a student's true intelligence. The case argued that there was a disproportionate number of African-American students identified as needing special education services (EMR program services). The court plaintiff Larry P. argued that IQ tests were **biased** against African-American students, which resulted in their placements in limiting educational settings. The defendant Riles argued that the prevalence of African-American students in the EMR classes was due to genetics and social and environmental factors. The court ultimately ruled that the IQ tests were discriminatory and resulted in the disproportionate placement of African-American students in the EMR setting. It was determined that these particular assessments were **culturally biased**, and the students' performances would be more accurately measured using adaptive behavior assessments, diagnostic tests, observations, and other assessments.

Diana v. State Board of Education

Diana v. State Board of Education (1970) is a court case that examined the case of a student who was placed in special education after results of the Stanford Binet Intelligence test indicated she had a mild case of "mental retardation." This class-action lawsuit was developed on behalf of nine **Mexican-American children**, arguing that IQ scores were not an adequate measurement to determine special education placement in the EMR setting. The case argued that Mexican-American children might be at a disadvantage because the IQ tests were written and administered in English. This might possibly constitute **discrimination**. The plaintiffs in the case argued that IQ scores were not a valid measurement because the children might have been unable to comprehend the test written in English. In the conclusive results of this case, the court ordered children to be tested in their primary language, if it was not English. As a result of this case, IQ tests were no longer used as the sole assessments for determining **special education placement**. There was also increased focus on **cultural and linguistic diversity** in students.

Winkelman v. Parma City Board of Education

This court case began as an argument against a **free and appropriate public education** as required by the Individuals with Disabilities Education Act (IDEA). The parents of Jacob Winkelman believed their son was not provided with a FAPE in his special education setting in Parma City Schools. The disagreement became about whether or not children can be **represented by their parents** per IDEA law in federal court. The U.S Court of Appeals for the Sixth Circuit argued that IDEA protected the rights of the children and not the parents. In the end, the District Court ruled that parents could represent their children within disputes over a free and appropriate public education as constituted by IDEA. Ultimately, this settled the question of whether or not **parents have rights under IDEA**, in addition to their children. The court case determined that parents play a significant role in the education of their children on Individualized Education Programs (IEPs) and are IEP team members. Therefore, parents are entitled to litigate *pro se* for their children.

Honig v. Doe

Honig v. Doe (1998) was a Supreme Court case examining the violation of the **Education for All Handicapped Children Act** (EAHCA, an earlier version of the Individuals with Disabilities Education Act) against the California School Board. The offense occurred when a child was suspended for a violent behavior outburst that was related to his disability. The court case centered on two plaintiffs. Both were diagnosed with an Emotional Disturbance and qualified for special education under EAHCA. Following the violent incident, the school suspended the students and recommended them for expulsion. The plaintiff's case argued that the suspension/expulsion went against the **stay-put provision of EAHCA**, which states that children with disabilities must remain in their current educational placements during review proceedings unless otherwise agreed upon by both parents and educational representatives. The defendant argued that the violence of the situation marked an exception to the law. The court determined that schools are able to justify the placement removal of a student when maintaining a **safe learning environment** outweighs a student's right to a free and appropriate public education.

Pennsylvania Association for Retarded Children v. Commonwealth of Pennsylvania

The Commonwealth of Pennsylvania was accused by the Pennsylvania Association for Retarded Children (PARC 1971), now known as the Arc of Pennsylvania, of denying a **free and appropriate public education** to students with disabilities. The Commonwealth of Pennsylvania was accused of refusing to educate students who had not met the "mental age of 5." The groups argued before the District Court of the Eastern District of Pennsylvania. This case was significant because PARC was one of the first institutions in the country to challenge the **placement of students with special needs**. The plaintiffs argued that all children should and would benefit from some sort of educational instruction and training. Ultimately, this was the beginning of instituting the state requirement of a free and appropriate public education (**FAPE**) for all children in public education from ages 6–21. The Commonwealth of Pennsylvania was tasked with providing a FAPE and sufficient education and training for all eligible children receiving special education. They could no longer deny students based on their mental ages. This triggered other state institutions to make similar decisions and led to the creation of similar federal policies in the **Education for All Handicapped Children Act** (1974).

1990 Amendments to the IDEA

The **Individuals with Disabilities Education Act (IDEA)** replaced the Education for All Handicapped Children Act in 1990. IDEA amendments changed the **age range** for children to receive special education services to ages 3–21. IDEA also changed the language of the law, changing the focus onto the **individuals with disabilities** rather than the **handicapped children**. Therefore, the focus shifted from the conditions or disabilities to the individual children and their needs. IDEA amendments also **categorized** different disabilities. IDEA 1997 increased the emphasis on the individualized education plans for students with disabilities and increased parents' roles in the educational decision-making processes for their children with disabilities. Part B of the 1997 amendment provided services to children ages 3–5, mandating that their learning needs be outlined in **Individualized Education Programs** or **Individualized Family Service Plans**. Part C of IDEA provided **financial assistance** to the families of infants and toddlers with disabilities. Part C states that educational agencies must provide **early intervention services** that focus on children's developmental and medical needs, as well as the needs of their families. Part C also gives states the option to provide services to children who are at risk for developmental disabilities.

Effect of the Individuals with Disabilities Education Improvement Act of 2004 on IDEA

In 2004, the Individuals with Disabilities Education Act implemented the **Individuals with Disabilities Education Improvement Act**. IDEA was reauthorized to better meet the needs of children in special education programs and children with special needs. As a result of these changes:

- Special educators are required to achieve Highly Qualified Teacher status and be certified in special education.
- Individualized Education Programs must contain measurable **annual goals** and descriptions of how progress toward the goals will be **measured and reported**.
- Schools or agencies must provide science or research-based **interventions** as part of the evaluation process to determine if children have specific learning disabilities. This may be done in addition to assessments that measure achievement or intelligence.

The changes made to require science or research-based interventions resulted in many districts implementing **Response to Intervention procedures**. These procedures meet the IDEA 2004 requirement of providing interventions in addition to achievement reports or intelligence tests on the Individualized Education Programs for children with disabilities.

Development of Educational Laws Like Goals 2000 and No Child Left Behind

President Bill Clinton signed the **National Educational Goals Act**, also known as Goals 2000, into effect in the 1990s to trigger standardized educational reform. The act focused on **outcomes-based education** and was intended to be completed by the year 2000. The goals of this act included ensuring that children are ready to learn by the time they start school, increasing high school graduation rates, demonstration of competency by students in grades 4, 8, and 12 in core content areas, and positioning the United States as first in the world in mathematics and science achievement. Goals 2000 was withdrawn when President George W. Bush implemented the **No Child Left Behind Act (NCLB)** in 2001. NCLB also supported standards-based reform, and it mandated that states develop more **skills-based assessments**. The act emphasized state testing, annual academic progress, report cards, and increased teacher qualification standards. It also outlined changes in state funding. NCLB required schools to meet **Adequate Yearly Progress (AYP)**. AYP was measured by results of achievement tests taken by students in each school district, and consequences were implemented for school districts that missed AYP during consecutive years.

Every Student Succeeds Act of 2015

NCLB was replaced in 2015 by the Every Student Succeeds Act (**ESSA**). ESSA built upon the foundations of NCLB and emphasized **equal opportunity** for students. ESSA currently serves as the main K–12 educational law in the United States. ESSA affects students in public education, including students with disabilities. The purpose of ESSA is to provide a **quality education** for all students. It also aims to address the achievement of **disadvantaged students**, including students living in

19

poverty, minority groups, students receiving special education services, and students with limited English language skills. ESSA determined that states may decide educational plans as long as they follow the government's framework. ESSA also allows states to develop their own educational standards and mandates that the curriculum focus on preparing students for post-secondary educations or careers. The act requires students to be tested annually in math and reading during grades 3–8 and once in high school. Students must also be tested in science once in elementary school, middle school, and high school. **School accountability** was also mandated by ESSA. The act requires states to have plans in place for any schools that are underperforming.

ESL Rights for Students and Parents

As public schools experience an influx of English as a Second Language (ESL) students, knowledge of their **rights** becomes increasingly important. The **Every Student Succeeds Act (ESSA)** of 2015 addresses funding discrepancies for ESL students and families. ESSA allocates funds to schools and districts where low-income families comprise 40% or more of the enrollment. This is intended to assist with ESL students who are underperforming or at risk for underperforming. ESSA also provides funding for ESL students to become English proficient and find academic success. However, in order for schools and districts to receive this funding, they must avoid discrimination, track ESL student progress, assess ESL student English proficiency, and notify parents of their children's ESL status. Avoiding discrimination includes preventing the over-identification of ESL students for special education services. The referral and evaluation process must be carried out with caution to ensure that students' perceived disabilities are actual deficits and not related to their English language learning abilities.

Rehabilitation Act of 1973

The Rehabilitation Act of 1973 was the law that preceded IDEA 1975. The Rehab Act serves to protect the rights of people with disabilities in several ways.

- It protects people with disabilities against discrimination relating to **employment**.
- It provides students with disabilities equal access to the **general education curriculum** (Section 504).

Americans with Disabilities Act of 1990 (ADA)

The Americans with Disabilities Act (1990) also protects the rights of people with disabilities.

- The ADA provides **equal employment** for people with disabilities. This means employers must provide reasonable accommodations for people with disabilities in their job and work environments.
- It provides **access** for people with disabilities to both public and private places open to the public (i.e. access ramps and automatic doors).
- It provides **telecommunications access** to people with disabilities. This ensures people with hearing and speech disabilities can communicate over the telephone and Internet.

Elementary and Secondary Education Act (ESEA)

The Elementary and Secondary Education Act (ESEA) also protects the rights of people with disabilities.

- Passed by President Johnson in 1965, ESEA was part of the president's "War on Poverty." The law sought to allow **equal access to a quality education**.
- ESEA extended more funding to secondary and primary schools and emphasized high **standards and accountability**.
- This law was authorized as **No Child Left Behind** (2001) under President Bush, then reauthorized as the **Every Student Succeeds Act** (ESSA) under President Obama.

Section 504

A Section 504 Plan comes from the civil rights law, Section 504 of the Rehabilitation Act of 1973, and protects the rights of individuals with disabilities. A 504 Plan is a formal plan or blueprint for how the school will provide services to a student with a disability. This essentially removes barriers for individuals with disabilities by ensuring that **appropriate services** are provided to meet their special needs. A 504 Plan includes:

- **Accommodations**: A 504 Plan includes accommodations a student with a disability may need to be successful in a regular education classroom. For example, a student with ADHD may need to sit near the front of the room to limit distractions.
- **Related Services**: A 504 Plan includes related services, such as speech therapy or occupational therapy, a student may need to be successful in the general education classroom.
- **Modifications**: Although it is rare for a 504 Plan to include modifications, sometimes they are included. Modifications change what the student is expected to do, such as being given fewer homework assignments.

504 Plans vs. Individualized Education Programs

- A 504 Plan and an Individualized Education Program are similar in that they serve as a blueprint for a student with a disability. However, a 504 Plan serves as a blueprint for how the student will have **access to school**, whereas the IEP serves as a blueprint for a student's **special education experience**.
- A 504 Plan helps level the playing field for a student with a disability by providing services and changes to the **learning environment**. An IEP provides individualized special education and related services to meet the **unique needs of a student with a disability**. Both IEPs and 504 Plans are provided at no cost to parents.
- The 504 Plan was established under the **Rehabilitation Act of 1973** as a civil rights law. The Individualized Education Program was established under the **Individuals with Disabilities Education Act** (1975 and amended in 2004).
- Unlike an IEP, a 504 Plan does **not** have to be a planned, written document. An IEP is a **planned, written document** that includes unique annual learning goals and describes related services for the student with a disability.

Informed Parental Consent

The Individuals with Disabilities Education Act (IDEA) requires that parents be **informed** before a student is evaluated for special education services. IDEA mandates that a school district receive **parental consent** to initiate an evaluation of a student for special education services. Consent means the school district has fully informed the parent of their intentions or potential reasons for evaluation of the student. Legally, the request must be written in the parent's native language. This consent does not mean the parent gives consent for a student's placement in special education. In order for a student to be initially placed in special education or receive special education services, parental consent must be given for this issue separately. At any time, parents can withdraw consent for special education placement or special education services. Schools are able to file **due process** if they disagree with the parental withdrawal of consent. Parents also have a right to consent to parts of a student's Individualized Education Program (IEP), but not necessarily all of the IEP. Once parental consent is granted for all parts of the IEP, it can be implemented.

Tiers of the Response to Intervention Model

- **Tier 1: High Quality Classroom Instruction, Screening, and Group Interventions**: In Tier 1, all students are screened using universal screening and/or the results of statewide assessments. Students identified as at risk receive supplemental instruction. Students who make adequate progress are returned to their regular instruction. Students who do not make adequate progress move to Tier 2.
- **Tier 2: Targeted Interventions**: These interventions are designed to improve the progress of the students who did not make adequate progress in Tier 1. Targeted instruction is usually in the areas of reading and math and does not last longer than one grading period.
- **Tier 3: Intensive Interventions and Comprehensive Evaluation**: Students who are not successful in Tier 2 move on to Tier 3. They receive intensive interventions that target their specific deficits. Students who do not meet progress goals during intensive interventions are referred to receive comprehensive evaluations and are considered to be eligible for special education under IDEA.

Stakeholders in Special Education

Stakeholders that play roles in educating students with disabilities include the students, parents, general educators, administrators, and community members. Students should receive an educational **curriculum** based on strict standards, such as the Common Core Content Standards. This ensures that they receive good educational foundations from which to grow and expand upon during their school careers. Parents, legal guardians, and sometimes agencies act in the best interests of their children. If they do not think the Individualized Education Programs suit the needs of their children, they can request **due process hearings** in court. FAPE and LRE ensure that students are educated alongside peers in general education classrooms by general educators. General educators collaborate with special educators to create **successful inclusion classrooms**. When inclusion is done successfully, the students with disabilities meet their IEP goals.

Information to Be Evaluated During Multi-Factored Evaluations or Evaluation Team Reports

Multi-Factored Evaluations are processes required by the Individuals with Disabilities Education Act to determine if a student is eligible for special education. When a student is suspected of having a disability, the parent or school district can initiate the evaluation process. **Student information** that is evaluated in a Multi-Factored Evaluation includes background information, health information, vision testing, hearing testing, social and emotional development, general intelligence, past and current academic performance, communication needs, gross and fine motor abilities, results of aptitude or achievement tests, academic skills, and current progress toward Individualized Education Program (IEP) goals. Progress reporting on IEP goals is only appropriate during an annual MFE when a student has already qualified for special education services. The purpose of an MFE is to provide **comprehensive information** about a student for professionals working with the student. An MFE also helps determine what academic or behavioral **goals** or related services might be appropriate for a student with disabilities.

Free and Appropriate Public Education Components

The Individuals with Disabilities Education Act (IDEA) defines free and appropriate public education (FAPE) as an educational right for children with disabilities in the United States. FAPE stands for:

- **Free**: All students found eligible for special education services must receive free services, expensed to the public instead of the parents.
- **Appropriate**: Students are eligible for educations that are appropriate for their specific needs, as stated in their Individualized Education Programs (IEPs).
- **Public**: Students with disabilities have the right to be educated in public schools.
- **Education**: An education must be provided to any school-aged child with a disability. Education and services are defined in a student's IEP.

Ideally, FAPE components are put in place in order to guarantee the best education possible that also suits the individual needs of a student with a disability. FAPE should take place in the least restrictive environment, or the environment with the fewest barriers to learning for the individual student with a disability.

Multi-Factored Evaluation or Evaluation Team Report

A Multi-Factored Evaluation (**MFE**), sometimes referred to as an Evaluation Team Report (**ETR**), serves as a snapshot of a child's abilities, strengths, and weaknesses. An MFE is conducted to determine a student's eligibility for special education. Once a student with a disability qualifies for special education, an MFE is conducted at least every three years after the initial MFE date. MFEs are conducted for students ages 3 to 21 who are on IEPs. The purpose of the MFE is to influence a student's **Individualized Education Program**. An MFE reports on a student's **current abilities** and how the disability may affect **educational performance**. MFEs can also determine if a student qualifies for related services, such as occupational therapy or speech-language therapy. An MFE can be requested by a parent or school district when a child is suspected of having a disability. The school district typically has 30 days or less to respond to a parental request to evaluate a student, giving consent or refusal for an evaluation. While initial MFEs are conducted as a means to determine special education qualification, annual MFEs are conducted to address any changes in the needs or services of a student already receiving special education services.

Least Restrictive Environments to Deliver Special Education Services

Special education services are delivered to students that qualify with a **disability** defined by the Individuals with Disabilities Education Act (IDEA). IDEA law also requires that students who qualify for special education must receive special education services in **least restrictive environments** that provide the fewest barriers to their learning. A student's most appropriate instructional setting is written out in the **Individualized Education Program (IEP)**. Some special education instructional settings include:

- no instructional setting
- mainstream setting
- resource room
- self-contained classroom
- homebound instruction

23

With **no instructional setting**, students participate in the general education curriculum but may receive related services, such as speech-language therapy or occupational therapy. In the **mainstream setting**, students are instructed in the general education classroom for most or part of the day and provided with special education supports, accommodations, modifications, and related services. A **resource room** is an environment where students receive remedial instruction when they cannot participate in the general curriculum for one or more subject areas. A **self-contained classroom** is a setting for students who need special education and related services for more than 50% of the day. **Homebound instruction** is for students who are homebound or hospital bound for more than four consecutive weeks.

Purpose of Special Education

Special education is specially designed instruction delivered to meet the individual needs of children with disabilities. Special education includes a free and appropriate education in the least restrictive environment. In the past, a special education model might consist of a self-contained classroom of students with special needs whose needs were addressed in that setting. Today, students who qualify for special education must receive instruction in **free and appropriate settings**. This means they receive special education services in settings that provide the **fewest barriers** to their learning. The most appropriate setting varies, depending on the student and the disability. The purpose of special education is to ensure that the unique needs of children with disabilities are addressed. In the public school setting, the Individuals with Disabilities Education Act mandates that students with disabilities receive free and appropriate public educations. The goal of special education is to create **fair environments** for students with special needs to learn. Ideally, the settings should enable students to learn to their fullest potential.

Due Process Rights Available to Parents and Legal Guardians

When parents or legal guardians and school districts cannot agree on components of a student with a disability's Individualized Education Program (IEP), parents and legal guardians have a right to **due process**. Due process is a legal right under the Individuals with Disabilities Education Act (IDEA) that usually involves the school district violating a legal rule. Examples of these violations include a school district not running an IEP meeting, failing to conduct a tri-annual evaluation, or failing to implement a student's IEP. Disputes often involve a student's instructional placement, appropriate accommodations or modifications, related services, or changes to IEPs. School districts' due process policies vary depending on the district. IDEA, however, mandates that a **due process legal form** be completed by the parent or legal guardian in order to move forward. This form must be completed within two years of a dispute. **Mediation**, or the process of coming to an agreement before filing due process, can be a solution to the dispute. IEP meetings, even when it is not time for an annual review, are also appropriate options for resolving a dispute before filing due process.

Purpose of Mediation in Lieu of a Parent or Legal Guardian Filing for Due Process

Mediation is a process used to address a dispute prior to a parent or legal guardian filing for due process. The purpose of mediation is to **resolve a dispute** between the parent or legal guardian of a student with a disability and the school district. Disputes occur when the parent or legal guardian does not agree with an IEP component, such as what related services are provided or the way a student's IEP is being implemented. Mediation is not a parent or legal guardian's legal right, but school districts often support mediation to offset a **due process filing**. Mediation involves the attempt to resolve a dispute and includes a meeting between the parent or legal guardian, school district member, and a neutral third party, such as a mediator provided by the state. States have lists of **mediators** available for these situations. Agreements that come out of the mediation process are put into writing and, if appropriate, put into a student's IEP. Disagreements can continue to be mediated, or the decision may be made to file due process. Prior to mediation, parents or legal guardians and school districts have the option of holding IEP meetings (outside of annual meetings) to resolve disputes.

Maintaining Confidentiality and Privacy of Student Records

Similar to the Health Insurance Portability and Accountability Act of 1966 (HIPAA), **FERPA** is a law that protects privacy. However, FERPA is specific to the privacy of students. The FERPA law applies to any school or agency that receives funds from the U.S. Department of Education. This ensures that schools or agencies cannot share any confidential information about a student without a parent or student's written consent. **Student educational records** can be defined as records, files, documents, or other materials which contain a student's personal information. Individualized **Education Programs** and **Evaluation Team Reports (ETRs)** are examples of private documents under the FERPA law. The responsibility of a school covered by FERPA is to maintain confidentiality and privacy. The members of an IEP team, such as special educators, related service professionals, general educators, or other professionals, cannot share any identifying, private information about a student. Information addressing the needs of individual students found on an IEP, Evaluation Team Report, or other identifying document must remain confidential unless express written consent is given by the parent or legal guardian.

Pre-Referral/Referral Process for Identifying and Placing a Student with a Disability

The purpose of a pre-referral process for a child with a suspected disability is to attempt **reasonable modifications and accommodations** before the child is referred for special education services. Schools often have **pre-referral teams** whose purpose is to identify the strengths and needs of a child, put reasonable strategies into action, and evaluate the results of this pre-referral intervention. If the results do not show any change, another intervention can be attempted, or the student can be referred for a special education evaluation.

If a child is suspected of having a disability and did not succeed with pre-referral interventions, the school or parent can request an **evaluation**. During the evaluation process, the school compiles information to see if the student needs special education or related services. This information is used to determine if the student's disability is affecting school performance and if the student qualifies for special education. The evaluation lists and examines the student's strengths, weaknesses, and development and determines what supports the student needs in order to learn. An evaluation must be completed before special education services can be provided.

Role of a School Psychologist in the Special Education

School psychologists are certified members of school teams that **support the needs of students and teachers**. They help students with overall academic, social, behavioral, and emotional success. School psychologists are trained in data collection and analysis, assessments, progress monitoring, risk factors, consultation and collaboration, and special education services. In special education, school psychologists may work directly with students and collaborate with teachers, administrators, parents, and other professionals working with particular students. They may also be involved in counseling students' parents, the Response to Intervention process, and performing initial evaluations of students who are referred for special education services. School psychologists also work to improve academic achievement, promote positive behavior and health by implementing school-wide programs, support learning needs of diverse learners, maintain safe school environments, and strengthen and maintain good school-parent relationships.

Overrepresentation of Students from Diverse Backgrounds

Disproportionate representation occurs when there is not an equal representation of students from different **cultural and linguistic backgrounds** identified for special education services. Students from different cultural and linguistic groups should be identified for special education services in similar proportions. This ensures that no one group is **overrepresented** and **overidentified as having special needs** due to their cultural or linguistic differences. Disproportionality can occur based on a child's sex, language proficiency, receipt of free and reduced lunch, or race and ethnicity. Historically, most disproportionality has been a civil rights issue and due to a child's cultural or linguistic background. Recently, the focus has been on the disproportional number of students who spend time in special education classrooms instead of being educated alongside regularly educated peers.

The referral process, **Response to Intervention (RTI)**, provides safeguards against disproportionality. The RTI process requires instruction and intervention catered to the unique, specific needs of the individual student. The purpose of RTI is not the identification of a disability or entitlement to services. Instead, it focuses on data used to make educational decisions about individuals, classrooms, schools, or districts. Models like RTI address disproportionate representation, but they are not perfect.

Types of Disability Categories

Specific Learning Disabilities (SLD) is the umbrella term for children who struggle with issues in their abilities to read, write, speak, listen, reason, or do math. **Other Health Impairment (OHI)** is another umbrella term for a disability that limits a child's strength, energy, or alertness. **Autism Spectrum Disorder (ASD)** is a disability that mostly affects a child's social and communication skills, and sometimes behavior. **Emotional Disturbance (ED)** is a disability category for a number of mental disorders. **Speech or Language Impairment** covers children with language impairments. **Visual Impairment or Blindness** is a disability category for children with visual impairments that significantly impair their abilities to learn. **Deafness**, **Hearing Impairment**, and **Deaf-Blindness** cover children diagnosed with these disabilities. Children with **Orthopedic Impairments** have impairments to their bodies. An **Intellectual Disability** is the diagnosis for students with below-average intellectual abilities. **Traumatic Brain Injury (TBI)** covers children who have suffered from TBIs. A diagnosis of **Multiple Disabilities** means a child has more than one disability defined by IDEA.

Interventions for Students with Physical Disabilities

A physical disability refers to any disability that limits **gross mobility** and prevents **normal body movement**. For example, muscular dystrophy is a physical disability that weakens the muscles of the human body over time. Students with physical disabilities require early interventions before grade school, if applicable. When students with physical disabilities enter grade school, they may receive interventions and related services if they qualify for special education and receive **Individualized Education Programs** or **504 Plans**. When physical disabilities do not affect the students' academic success, they may be put on 504 Plans to receive appropriate related services, accommodations, or modifications. When physical disabilities are present with other disabilities, or the physical disabilities affect academic performance, students may be put on Individualized Education Programs. They may also receive appropriate related services, accommodations, and modifications. Teachers, intervention specialists, physiotherapists, occupational therapists, and speech language pathologists are all team members that work with students with physical disabilities by assisting and implementing appropriate accommodations, modifications, and related services.

Dyslexia and Dysgraphia Disorders

Students with dyslexia are eligible for special education with a specific learning disability under the Individuals with Disabilities Education Act if their educational performances are significantly impacted by their disabilities. **Dyslexia** is a permanent condition that makes it difficult for people to read. This affects reading accuracy, fluency, and comprehension. Dyslexia also generalizes to difficulties in the content areas of writing, mathematics, spelling, and reading comprehension. Children who have dyslexia often have difficulties with **phonemic awareness skills** and **decoding**. It is not a disability that affects vision or the way people see letters. Dyslexia may coexist with other conditions such as **dysgraphia**, which is a disorder that causes issues with written expression. With dysgraphia, children often struggle with holding pencils and writing letters accurately. It is difficult for students with dysgraphia to distinguish shapes, use correct letter spacing, read maps, copy text, understand spelling rules, and more.

Behavioral Issues for Students with Autism

Autism is a **spectrum disorder**, which means the characteristics associated with the disability vary depending on the student. However, there are common repetitive and patterned behaviors associated with communication and social interactions for this population of students.. Students with autism may demonstrate delayed or different speech patterns, the inability to understand body language or facial expressions, and the inability to exhibit appropriate speech patterns, body language, or facial expressions. In a classroom environment, students with autism may demonstrate **repetitive behaviors** that are distracting, such as hand flapping or making vocalizations. Some students with autism demonstrate **preoccupation** with doing activities, tasks, or routines in certain ways. This preoccupation can lead to difficulties when the students are asked to make changes to the activities, tasks, or routines. Furthermore, some students with autism prefer to **participate** in a limited range of activities and may get upset when asked to participate in activities outside of their self-perceived ranges. Repetitive behaviors may translate into obsessions or excessive knowledge relating to one particular topic. Extreme interests in one topic can turn into disruptions when students with autism are asked to speak or write about different topics.

Effect of Hearing Loss on Language Development

Hearing language is part of learning language. Children with **hearing loss** miss out on sounds associated with language, and this can affect their listening, speaking, reading, social skills, and overall school success. Hearing loss can sometimes lead to delayed speech and language, learning disabilities in school, insecurities, and issues with socialization and making friends. Children with hearing loss may:

- have trouble learning abstract vocabulary (i.e. since, before).
- omit article words in sentences (i.e. a, an).
- fall behind on core components of learning and development without early interventions.
- have difficulty speaking in and/or understanding sentences.
- speak in shorter sentences.
- have difficulty including word endings (i.e. -ing, -s).
- have issues speaking clearly because they cannot accurately hear sounds.
- omit quiet sounds, like *p, sh,* or *f.*
- be unable to hear what their own voices sound like.

27

Children with hearing loss are more likely to fall behind in school due to their hearing deficits. They can easily fall behind without support from interventions, teachers, and their families. Early **hearing testing** is essential to ensure that interventions, such as sign language, can be introduced to promote school and life success for children with hearing loss.

Receptive Language Disorders

Children with receptive language disorders often demonstrate appropriate expressive language skills and hear and read at age-appropriate levels. They may seem like they are not paying attention or engaging in activities, or appear to have difficulties following or understanding directions. They may refrain from asking questions or interrupt frequently during activities, especially during read aloud activities. It may appear as if they are not listening, but children with receptive language disorders cannot perceive **meaning** from what they hear. Children with this disorder may consistently leave tasks incomplete unless the tasks are broken down into smaller steps. This is due to issues with directions, especially **verbal directions**. Children with receptive language disorders may not respond appropriately or at all to questions from peers or adults. Answers to comprehension questions, especially when texts are read aloud, may be off topic or incorrect. Children with receptive language disorders have trouble gathering and connecting meaning to what they hear. A receptive language disorder is not exclusively a learning disability. However, children who have receptive disorders may have learning disabilities.

Types of Disabilities

Medical disabilities include problems related to diseases, illnesses, and trauma. Medical disabilities can also include problems related to genetics. **Physical disabilities** include problems related to fine and gross motor skills and can include sensory input or sensory perception disorders. Medical and physical disabilities often manifest with other disabilities, such as **learning disabilities**. Medical disabilities, such as a student whose health issue affects educational performance, are usually categorized under the *Other Health Impaired* or *Traumatic Brain Injury* eligibility categories under the Individuals with Disabilities Education Act (IDEA). People with physical disabilities, such as cerebral palsy, can be eligible for special education under IDEA under the Orthopedic Impairment category. However, for both medical and physical disabilities to qualify, a student's medical or physical disability must **adversely affect educational performance**. For example, a student with cerebral palsy may not be eligible for special education or an Individualized Education Program if the disability does not affect educational performance. The student would receive accommodations and modifications under a 504 Plan.

Educational Implications of a Diagnosis of SLD, OHI, ASD, and ED

Students with **Specific Learning Disability** (SLD) may struggle with instruction in general education classrooms and require specific instruction fine-tuned to their individual needs. Their annual IEP goals may target specific skills that are not age appropriate but are appropriate to their unique learning needs. An **OHI (Other Health Impairment)** diagnosis can include children with ADHD, diabetes, HIV/AIDS, heart conditions, and more. Students with OHI receive accommodations for their unique health or educational needs on a case-by-case basis. Students with **Autism Spectrum Disorder (ASD)** may rely on the use of visuals or access to other ways to express feelings or communicate. Students with ASD may not respond to everyday conversations or classroom situations the same ways their peers do. They require supports to learn how to express their needs within the general education classroom. Students with **emotional disturbances (ED)** exhibit an inability to learn that is not due to intellectual, sensory, or health problems. Students with ED also exhibit inability to form and maintain appropriate relationships with peers and adults, demonstrate inappropriate behaviors, and may exhibit depression or general unhappiness.

Early Characteristics Indicating a Child Has a Specific Learning Disability

Early characteristics that indicate a specific learning disability (**SLD**) include factors like medical history, speech acquisition, problems with socialization, academic delays, and behavioral delays. Delays in certain milestones may indicate learning disabilities, but these delays may also be due to other causes. Premature birth, serious childhood illnesses, frequent ear infections, and sleep disorders are **medical factors** that can influence the development of learning disabilities. Children that develop SLDs may demonstrate early delays in **oral speech**. For example, late speech development, pronunciation problems, and stuttering may indicate SLDs, but these issues may also sometimes be addressed by individualized speech instruction. Students with SLDs may also have problems adjusting **socially**. They may demonstrate social skills that are not age appropriate. Depending on when the children enter academic settings, they may demonstrate academic delays compared to similar-aged peers. These delays are usually determined using formal and informal assessments in educational settings. **Behaviors** such as hyperactivity or difficulty following directions may also indicate a child has a SLD. However, these indicators do not definitely mean that a child has a learning disability, and some of the indicators overlap with characteristics of other disabilities.

Instructional Strategies for Teaching Students with Specific Learning Disabilities

While there is no one strategy that works effectively with all students with specific learning disabilities, there are some strategies that tend to produce **positive outcomes** for these students. Direct instruction, learning strategy instruction, and a multi-sensory approach are three large-scale interventions that can be used to promote student learning. **Direct instruction** is teacher-driven instruction that targets specific skills. Direct instruction is sometimes delivered in resource rooms. **Learning strategy instruction** is a method for teaching students with disabilities different tools and techniques useful for learning new content or skills. Learning strategy instruction includes techniques like chunking the content, sequencing tasks, and small group instruction. A **multi-sensory approach** ensures that students are receiving and interacting with new information and skills using more than one sense at a time. This approach is helpful for students with learning disabilities because it targets many different ways of learning.

Children with Emotional Disturbances

A diagnosis of an emotional disturbance can also be referred to as a **behavioral disorder** or **mental illness**. Causes of emotional disturbances are generally unclear. However, heredity, brain disorders, and diet are some factors that influence the development of emotional disturbances. Emotional disturbance is the general term for children with anxiety disorders, bipolar disorder, eating disorders, obsessive-compulsive disorder, or any other psychotic disorders. The Individuals with Disabilities Education Act states that emotional disturbances can affect children beyond emotion and make them eligible for **special education** with this diagnosis. Children's cognitive, physical, or social behaviors may also be affected. Indicators of emotional disturbances include hyperactivity, aggression, withdrawal, immaturity, and academic difficulties. While many children demonstrate these indicators throughout their development, a strong indicator of an emotional disturbance is a **prolonged demonstration** of these behaviors. Children who have emotional disorders demonstrate behaviors associated with particular disorders. For example, a child with obsessive-compulsive disorder will demonstrate uncontrolled, reoccurring thoughts and behaviors.

Issues Students with ED Experience in the Instructional Setting

Students with the diagnosis of emotional disturbance (ED) as defined by the Individuals with Disabilities Education Act require **emotional and behavioral support** in the classroom. Students with ED may also require **specialized academic instruction** in addition to behavioral and emotional support. The amount of support given varies according to the needs of individual students. These students also need **scaffolded instruction** in social skills, self-awareness, self-esteem, and self-control. Students with ED often exhibit behaviors that impede their learning or the learning of others. **Positive Behavioral Support (PBS)** is a preventative instructional strategy that focuses on promoting positive behaviors in students. With PBS, teachers or other professionals make changes to students' environments in order to decrease problem behaviors. PBS involves the process of collecting information on the behavior, identifying positive ways to support the behavior, and implementing a support to decrease the behavior. Supports can be implemented schoolwide or in the classroom. However, for students with ED, **classroom supports** are more effective because they can be individualized.

Signs Indicating a Child Has a Speech or Language Impairment

Speech and language impairments, sometimes referred to as **communication disorders**, are disabilities recognized by the Individuals with Disabilities Education Act. Students diagnosed with communication disorders are eligible for special education if they qualify for services. Early indicators of communication disorders include but are not limited to:

- not smiling or interacting with others.
- lack of babbling or cooing in infants.
- lack of age-appropriate comprehension skills.
- speech that is not easily understood.
- issues with age-appropriate syntax development.
- issues with age-appropriate social skills.
- deficits in reading and writing skills.

Stuttering, beginning or ending words with incorrect sounds, and hearing loss are also indicators of possible communication disorders. These are symptoms of communication disorders, but they can also be linked to other disabilities, such as hearing impairments or autism. A prolonged demonstration of these indicators may suggest communication disorders. However, children can demonstrate delays and self-correct as they grow.

Qualifications to Be Eligible for Special Education Under the Category of OHI

The category of **Other Health Impaired** (OHI) under the Individuals with Disabilities Education Act (IDEA) indicates that a child has **limited strength, vitality, or alertness**. This includes hyper-alertness or hypo-alertness to environmental stimuli. In order to be eligible for special education under this category according to IDEA, the disability must **adversely affect educational performance**. It must also be due to **chronic or acute health problems**, such as attention deficit disorder (ADD), attention deficit hyperactivity disorder (ADHD), diabetes, epilepsy, heart conditions, hemophilia, lead poisoning, leukemia, nephritis, rheumatic fever, sickle cell anemia, or Tourette's Syndrome. It is important to note that in order to be eligible under this category, the disability must be affecting a child's academic performance. Since the OHI category encompasses a number of different disabilities, teachers and parents must rely on a student's Individualized Education Program to ensure that individual academic needs are met and appropriate accommodations and modifications are provided.

Educational Implications and Limitations of Students Eligible for Special Education

According to the Individuals with Disabilities Education Act (IDEA), students who are eligible for special education under the category of **Intellectual Disability** have significantly lower intellectual abilities, along with adaptive behavior deficits. Previously, intellectual disability was referred to as mental retardation. In 2010, President Obama signed **Rosa's Law**, which changed the term to *intellectual disability*. The definition of the disability category remained unchanged. Educational implications of a diagnosis of an intellectual disability differ depending on students' needs as determined by their Individualized Education Programs (IEPs). Students with intellectual disabilities often display **limitations to mental functioning** in skills like communication, self-care, and social skills (adaptive behavior). In many cases, these skills must be addressed in the educational environments in addition to any academic skill deficits. Learning adaptive behaviors and academic skills takes longer for students with intellectual disabilities, so their special education placements depend upon what environments are least restrictive. This depends on the individual student and is determined in the IEP.

Components of the Multiple Disability Eligibility Category According to IDEA

A diagnosis of multiple disabilities according to the Individuals with Disabilities Education Act (IDEA) indicates two or more disabilities occurring simultaneously. The difference between a diagnosis of intellectual disability and **multiple disabilities** is that students with multiple disabilities present with such **severe educational needs** that they cannot be accommodated in special education settings that address only one disability. Students with multiple disabilities require assistance for more than one disability. Their educational performances are adversely affected by their disabilities. Placement in special education programs is determined by students' **least restrictive environments** and defined in their **Individualized Education Programs**. The multiple disability category does not encompass deaf-blindness, which has its own category under IDEA. Students with multiple disabilities often present with communication deficits and difficulties, mobility challenges, deficits in adaptive behavior, and the need for one-on-one instruction or assistance when performing daily activities.

Qualifications to Receive Special Education for Orthopedic Impairment

A student who qualifies to receive special education under the Individuals with Disabilities Education Act category for **Orthopedic Impairment** has a disability that adversely affects educational performance. This includes children with congenital anomalies, impairments caused by disease, or impairments from other causes, such as cerebral palsy or amputations. An orthopedic impairment alone does not qualify a student for special education and an Individualized Education Program. Once a student's educational performance is proven to be affected by the orthopedic impairment, the student can be eligible for special education and placed on an **IEP**. The IEP determines the student's least restrictive environment, individualized goals for academic skills or adaptive behavior, and any appropriate accommodations or modifications. Students with orthopedic impairments whose educational performances are not affected may receive accommodations and modifications on **504 Plans** if appropriate for their disabilities. Strategies for instruction should be determined and implemented on a case-by-case basis, as the orthopedic impairment category covers a broad range of disabilities.

Strategies Facilitating Learning in Students with Speech or Language Impairments

In order to teach students with speech or language impairments, also referred to as **communication disorders**, special educators and professionals can use certain strategies to ensure learning takes place. Teachers and other professionals can use the **strategies** listed below:

- Use visuals and concrete examples to help students with communication disorders take in new information visually. Link the visuals with spoken words or phrases.
- Use visuals or photographs to introduce or reinforce vocabulary.
- Use repetition of spoken words to introduce or reinforce vocabulary.
- Model conversational and social skills, which helps students with communication disorders become familiar with word pronunciation.
- Speak at a slower rate when necessary, especially when presenting new information.
- Consistently check for understanding.
- Be aware that communication issues may sometimes result in other issues, such as behavioral or social skill issues.
- Pair actions and motions with words to emphasize meaning, especially for students with receptive language disorders.

Determining If a Child May Have an Intellectual Disability

Students diagnosed with intellectual disabilities (**ID**) demonstrate deficits in academic skills, abstract thinking, problem solving, language development, new skill acquisition, and retaining information. Students with intellectual disabilities do not adequately meet developmental or social milestones. They demonstrate **deficits in functioning** with one or more basic living skills. Students with intellectual disabilities struggle conceptually and sometimes demonstrate delays in language development. They may also have difficulties with time and money concepts, short-term memory, time management skills, pre-academic and academic skills, planning, and strategizing. Socially, this population of students may also grasp concrete concepts over abstract concepts, but in a process that is significantly behind their similar-aged, regular education peers. Students with ID demonstrate poor social judgement and decision-making skills because they have trouble understanding social cues and rules. These students also tend to struggle with self-care skills, household tasks, and completing tasks that may be easy for similar-aged peers.

Promoting a Positive Educational Performance for Students with Intellectual Disabilities

Students with intellectual disabilities often present skills that are far below the skill levels of similar-aged peers. Due to skill deficits in academic, behavioral, and social skills, these students require **specialized instruction** to address specific skills. The skills addressed vary depending on the needs of each individual student. An effective strategy for promoting a positive educational performance is to collect observations and data on the academic, behavioral, and social skill levels of the individual student. Teachers usually work with related services members, like speech language pathologists, to address needs and implement educational interventions that work for this population of students. These students can benefit from **communication interventions** focused on interactions the students may have with adults and peers. Students may benefit from augmentative communication devices, visual activity schedules, visual supports, and computer-based instruction to teach communication and social skills. Students with ID may also require **behavioral interventions** to teach appropriate behaviors or decrease negative behaviors. They may also benefit from increased **peer interactions** through structured social groups in order to promote appropriate communication skills.

Early Indications of Visual Impairment or Blindness

A visual impairment ranges from low vision to blindness. The Individuals with Disabilities Education Act defines a **visual impairment** as an impairment in vision that is great enough to affect a child's educational performance. **Blindness** is defined as a visual acuity of 20/200 or less in the dominant eye. Some people diagnosed with blindness still have minimal sight. Early indicators of a visual impairment or blindness for children include:

- holding things closely to their eyes or faces.
- experiencing fatigue after looking at things closely.
- misaligned eyes or squinting.
- tilting heads or covering eyes to see things up close or far away.
- demonstrating clumsiness.
- appearing to see better during the day.

Students who are diagnosed with visual impairments or blindness who are also eligible for special education benefit the most from early interventions, especially when the impairments are present with other disabilities. Appropriate interventions vary based on each student and whether or not the impairments are paired with other disabilities. Modifications, such as magnified text, Braille, auditory support, and text-tracking software, also help level the learning plane for these students.

Early Communication and Social Skill Delays in Students with ASD

Students with delays in communication development often need and receive some type of assistance or instruction with communication and social skills. For students with **Autism Spectrum Disorder (ASD)**, the need for communication and social skill instruction varies depending on the individual student. Early intervention for these students is key, as communication difficulties are an early symptom of Autism Spectrum Disorder. Key characteristics of **early communication difficulties** for a student with ASD may include not responding to his/her name, not pointing at objects of interest, avoiding eye contact, not engaging in pretend play, delayed speech or language skills, or repeating words or phrases. Children with ASD may also exhibit overreaction or underreaction to environmental stimuli. Key characteristics of **early social skill difficulties** for a student with ASD may include preferring to play alone, trouble understanding personal feelings or the feelings of others, not sharing interests with others, and difficulty with personal space boundaries. Infants with ASD may not respond to their names and demonstrate reduced babbling and reduced interest in people. Toddlers with ASD may demonstrate decreased interest in social interactions, difficulty with pretend play, and a preference for playing alone.

Characteristics of Social Skill Delays in Students with ASD

Autism Spectrum Disorder (ASD) is a disability that can affect a student's social, communication, and behavioral abilities. **Social skill delays and deficits** are common for students with ASD. Characteristics of social skill delays go hand-in-hand with **communication limitations** for students with ASD. This includes conversational focus on one or two narrow topics or ideas. This limits their conversations to one or two subject areas, and it is difficult for them to hold two-way conversations about things that do not interest them. Some students with ASD engage in repetitive language or echolalia or rely on standard phrases to communicate with others. Their **speech and language skills** may be delayed compared to their similar-aged peers. This may also affect their abilities to engage in effective, two-way conversations. The **nonverbal skills** of students with ASD may also be misinterpreted, such as avoiding eye contact while speaking or being spoken to.

Early Signs of a Child Having ASD

Early signs of **Autism Spectrum Disorder** (ASD) include impairments or delays in social interactions and communication, repetitive behaviors, limited interests, and abnormal eating habits. Students with ASD typically do not interact in conversations in the same ways as similar-aged peers without ASD. They may demonstrate inability to engage in pretend play and may pretend they don't hear when being spoken to. Hand flapping, vocal sounds, or compulsive interactions with objects are repetitive behaviors sometimes demonstrated by students with ASD. They may only demonstrate interest in talking about one topic or be interested in interacting with one object. They may also demonstrate self-injurious behavior or sleep problems, in addition to having a limited diet of preferred foods. **Early intervention** is key for these students in order to address and improve functioning. These students may also benefit from **applied behavior analysis** to target specific behaviors and require speech and language therapy, occupational therapy, social skills instruction, or other services geared toward improving intellectual functioning.

Low-Incidence Disabilities and High-Incidence Disabilities

Low-incidence disabilities account for up to 20% of all students' disabilities. Students with low-incidence disabilities have sometimes received assistance for their disabilities starting from an early age. This group includes students with intellectual disabilities and significant developmental delays. **Low-incidence disabilities** can include intellectual disabilities, multiple disabilities, hearing impairments, orthopedic impairments, other health impairments, visual impairments, autism, deaf-blindness, traumatic brain injury, and developmental delays. **High-incidence disabilities** account for up to 80% of all students' disabilities. Students with high-incidence disabilities present with academic, social, and/or behavioral problems and can often be held to the same standards as their regular education peers. Children with high-incidence disabilities may perform at the same capacities as their similar-aged peers but have deficits in reading, math, writing, handwriting, or maintaining attention. They may also present with limitations in communication, adaptive behavior, and social skills. Examples of high-incidence disabilities include speech and language impairments, learning disabilities, attention deficit hyperactivity disorder, emotional disorders, mild intellectual disabilities, certain spectrums of autism, and cognitive delays.

Sensory Processing Disorders

When a person experiences a deficit with handling sensory information interpreted by the brain, this is called a **sensory processing disorder (SPD)**. In brains without SPD, people can experience sensory input, and their brain receptors can interpret them to demonstrate appropriate reactions. In brains of people with SPD, the brains experience sensory input, but the brains' receptors are blocked, resulting in abnormal reactions. Previously known as a sensory integration disorder, SPD is not a disability specifically defined or eligible under the Individuals with Disabilities Education Act (IDEA). However, many students with disabilities defined by IDEA, like autism, also experience some sort of sensory processing disorder. Students with SPD may display **oversensitive or under-sensitive responses** to their environments, stimuli, and senses. Students with SPD may not understand physical boundaries, such as where their bodies are in space. They may bump into things and demonstrate clumsiness. These students may get upset easily, throw tantrums, demonstrate high anxiety, and not handle changes well.

Characteristics and Causes of ADHD and ADD

Children with **Attention Deficit Hyperactivity Disorder** (ADHD) may demonstrate hyperactivity, inattention, and impulsivity. However, they may demonstrate hyperactivity and inattention only or

34

hyperactivity and impulsivity. Children with **Attention Deficit Disorder** (ADD) demonstrate inattention and impulsivity, but not hyperactivity. Students with either ADHD or ADD may have difficulties with attention span, following instructions, and concentrating to the point that educational performance is affected. Since ADD and ADHD symptoms are common among children, their presence does not necessarily indicate that a child needs a diagnosis of ADD or ADHD. ADD and ADHD are not caused by certain environmental factors, such as diet or watching too much television. Symptoms may be exacerbated by these factors, but the real causes can be heredity, chemical imbalances, issues with brain functions, environmental toxins, or prenatal trauma, such as the mother smoking or drinking during pregnancy.

Importance of Adaptive Behavior Skills Instruction for Students with Disabilities

Adaptive behavior skills refer to age-appropriate behaviors that people need to live independently and function in daily life. **Adaptive behavior skills** include self-care skills, following rules, managing money, making friends, and more. For students with disabilities, especially severely limiting disabilities, adaptive behavior skills may need to be included in daily instruction. Adaptive behavior skills can be separated into conceptual skills, social skills, and practical life skills. **Conceptual skills** include academic concepts, such as reading, math, money, time, and communication skills. **Social skills** instruction focuses on teaching students to get along with others, communicate appropriately, and maintain appropriate behavior inside and outside the school environment. **Practical life skills** are skills needed to perform the tasks of daily living. Adaptive behavior assessments are useful in assessing what adaptive behavior skills need to be addressed for each student. These assessments are usually conducted using observations and questionnaires completed by parents, teachers, or students.

Effect of Environmental Factors on Social-Emotional Development

A person's **environment** has a large impact on social-emotional environment. Factors that impact a child's social-emotional development include:

- family relationships and environment.
- play-based learning.
- a nurturing environment.
- verbal skills.

Children who grow up with strong, solid family relationships in stable environments tend to develop appropriate **social-emotional skills**. Children who experience family or environmental stress and trauma, such as divorce or constant fighting, may demonstrate deficits in their social-emotional growth. **Play-based learning** fosters important skills and brain development when children observe adults demonstrating acceptable social behavior. In positive, nurturing environments, children learn by watching adults interacting appropriately with one another. They learn skills that foster social and emotional well-being. The first sounds infants hear are voices. Children first grasp a sense of spoken language in their home environments. Caregivers that speak to their children consistently help them develop **strong verbal skills**.

Physical Stages of Gross Motor Development in Children

Gross motor skills refer to larger motor skills that require movement of the body as a whole. Gross motor skills begin developing in **infancy** as children learn to crawl and walk. At ages **two to three**, children transition from toddling to walking, then learn to jump, run, hop, throw, catch, and push themselves in riding toys with their feet. Children ages **three to four** become skilled at stair climbing. They also jump higher and develop better upper body mobility. Additionally, they develop

35

the ability to ride a small bike or tricycle and kick large balls accurately. At ages **four to five**, children can go up and down stairs with ease. They also develop running mobility skills and speed and have more control when riding bikes or tricycles. Children ages **five to six** fine tune previously learned gross motor skills. They are more adept at physical play skills, such as those needed to play on jungle gyms or swings independently. Children in this age range demonstrate interest in organized sports and other extracurricular activities. Children develop and refine their gross motor skills as they grow. Sometimes a child will demonstrate a **delay** in a gross motor skill, but this does not always indicate a disability. Some disabilities are characterized by specific delays in gross motor skills. Parents and educators should be familiar with **gross motor skill milestones** in order to pinpoint any significant delays in students.

Fine Motor Abilities of Children

Fine motor skills are skills focused on smaller movements, usually involving the hands and fingers. Children ages **two to three** begin to make things using their hands, such as block towers. They can scribble with writing utensils and manipulate playdough. They demonstrate conceptual knowledge of basic puzzles, fitting appropriate pieces into their correct locations. At this age, children begin to demonstrate a right or left-hand dominance. Adjusting fasteners, such as buttons and snaps, independently dressing and undressing, and cutting paper with scissors are fine motor milestones for children ages **three to four**. These children also fine tune their eating skills and use larger writing tools, maintaining a specific grip instead of a grasp. Children ages **four to five** refine their fine motor skills. Their artistic skills become more refined as they become more confident in hand dominance and drawing. Children ages **five to seven** begin to demonstrate fine motor abilities, such as writing letters and numbers and creating shapes. They use utensils and writing tools with greater ease. Children in this age range can complete self-care tasks independently, such as teeth brushing. A child with a **fine motor delay** would demonstrate a significant deficit in one or more fine motor skills at one or more stages of development.

Classroom Strategies Promoting Social-Emotional Development and Growth

Classroom environments should emanate **positivity** and **growth**. Classrooms that promote **social-emotional development and growth** provide security for students and create environments where learning takes place. Teachers can promote social-emotional development and growth by creating predictable classroom routines with visual reminders, keeping classrooms free of dangerous objects and materials, and arranging for learning to take place in large and small groups. They can also rotate activities and materials to keep students engaged, provide appropriate materials for learning centers, and create opportunities for children to engage socially. Teachers can act as nurturing adults by encouraging social interactions and problem solving, modeling appropriate language and social skills, encouraging and validating children's thoughts and feelings, and using clear signals to indicate transitions between activities. Teachers should build community environments in their classrooms, build appropriate relationships with students by getting to know their strengths and weaknesses, and demonstrate good conflict resolution and problem-solving abilities.

Educational Implications of Instructing Children with ADHD or ADD

The Individuals with Disabilities Education Act (IDEA) does **not** recognize Attention Deficit Hyperactivity Disorder (ADHD) or Attention Deficit Disorder (ADD) in any of its 13 major disability categories. Students may be diagnosed with ADHD or ADD only by a physician, but this diagnosis is not enough to qualify the student for **special education services**. When ADHD or ADD are present with another disability, such as a learning disability, the student qualifies for special education services under the learning disability. A student whose ability to learn is affected by ADHD or ADD can receive services with a 504 Plan in place. Section 504 provides services for any child whose disability affects a major life activity and makes the child eligible for accommodations and modifications in the classroom. This ensures that the child receives appropriate **accommodations** and/or **modifications** in the learning environment in order to be successful. Parents who think a child's disability adversely affects educational functioning may request a formal evaluation to be performed by the school. If a child is found to qualify for special education services, the child receives services under the **Other Health Impaired** category of IDEA.

Effect of Emotional and Psychological Needs on Students with a Disabilities

When a child is diagnosed with a disability, educators often primarily focus on the educational implications. However, students with disabilities also have **emotional needs** associated with their disabilities. These needs vary by student and disability. Generally, students with disabilities struggle emotionally. Symptoms may include low self-esteem, anxiety, acting out, reduced intrinsic motivation, and physical symptoms like headaches. Educators, parents, and other professionals can manage the emotional needs of students with disabilities by talking about the disability diagnoses and educational implications of the diagnoses with the students. Educators can increase their **awareness** of how students might be feeling about the diagnoses and identify situations that may cause anxiety or acting out. Educators can also help by praising students consistently, even for small actions, which can help with confidence. Parents, educators, and other professionals can also work together to ensure that the students receive instruction in the most appropriate educational environments for their disabilities.

Determining Severe, Profound, and Mild Intellectual Disabilities

There are three levels of intellectual disabilities: severe, profound, and mild. Specific factors are used to determine whether a disability is severe, profound, or mild. Intellectual levels are measured using cognitive-based and research-based assessments. An **intellectual disability** is defined as having significant cognitive deficits to intellectual functioning, such as reasoning, problem solving, abstract thinking, and comprehension. A **mild to moderate intellectual disability (ID)** is the most common type of intellectual disability. People with mild to moderate ID can generally participate in independent living skills and learn practical life skills and adaptive behavior. People diagnosed with **severe intellectual disabilities** demonstrate major developmental delays. They struggle with simple routines and self-care skills. Additionally, they often understand speech but have trouble with expressive communication. People with **profound ID** cannot live independently and depend heavily on care from other people and resources. They are likely to have congenital disorders that affect their intellectual functioning.

Social Cognitive Learning Theory

Albert Bandura's social cognitive learning theory features four stages or processes of observational learning: attention, retention, production, and motivation. **Observational learning** is based on the idea that a person modifies behavior after being provided with a model for the behavior. Not to be confused with exact imitation of behavior, observational learning occurs when a behavior is witnessed then demonstrated at a later time as a result of witnessing the behavior. For example, a child learns how to hold eating utensils by watching an adult hold the utensils. **Attention** refers to a person paying attention to what is happening in the environment. In the **retention** stage, a person not only observes the behavior, but stores it in memory to perform later. **Production** requires the person to be physically and mentally able to reproduce the behavior. The **motivation** stage means the person must be motivated or have an incentive to reproduce the behavior. Students with disabilities may struggle with one or more of the observational stages as a characteristic of their disabilities. Limitations, such as attention difficulties, present barriers to appropriately moving through the observational learning processes.

Educational Implications of a Diagnosis of an Impairment

Speech or Language Impairment and **Visual Impairment or Blindness** adversely affect a student's educational performance. Students with Speech or Language Impairments and Visual Impairments or Blindness are provided with accommodations, modifications, and related services specific to their disabilities. Students with these impairments may be educated alongside peers and provided with related services outside of the general education classroom. Similar to these disabilities, the educational performances of students with **Deafness or Hearing Impairments** are also affected by their disabilities. Accommodations, modifications, and related services are provided based on the severity of the disability.

An **OI** severely impairs mobility or motor activity. Accommodations, modifications, and related services in the classroom environments may be appropriate for students with Orthopedic Impairments. Students with **ID**, such as students with Down Syndrome, often need supports in place for communication, self-care, and social skills. The educational implications of a student with **TBI** are unique to the individual and are therefore treated on a case by case basis. Students with **MD** have needs that cannot be met in any one program. Sometimes their needs are so great that they must be educated in partial inclusion or self-contained settings.

Autism Spectrum Disorder vs. Specific Learning Disabilities

Autism Spectrum Disorder (**ASD**) and learning disabilities can exist concurrently. Students with ASD may also have a lot in common with students with learning disabilities. However, ASD is a spectrum disorder that affects children in different ways. ASD is often confused with learning and attention issues, but students with ASD can have IQs ranging from significantly delayed to above average or gifted. Students with **learning disabilities** often have consistently lower IQs. Students with **attention issues** like Attention Deficit Hyperactivity Disorder also have varying needs, depending on if the ADHD exists with a learning disability or ASD. Students with learning disabilities and students with ASD may both have difficulties recognizing and reading nonverbal cues, staying organized, problem solving, and expressing themselves. They may also have issues with desiring or rejecting sensory input. These disabilities are different because ASD involves struggles with social understanding and communication, along with repetitive routines or behaviors. These struggles are not associated with students with learning disabilities.

Role of Cultural Competence in Schools and Special Education

Schools have a duty to abide by cultural competence in order to ensure avoidance of **cultural and linguistic bias**. Schools that demonstrate **cultural competence** have an appreciation of families and their unique backgrounds. Cultural competence is important because it assists with incorporating knowledge and appreciation of other cultures into daily practices and teaching. This helps increase the quality and effectiveness of how students with unique cultural and linguistic backgrounds are provided with services. It also helps produce better outcomes for these students. In special education, being culturally competent means being aware of cultural and linguistic differences, especially when considering children for the identification process. Adapting to the **diversity and cultural contexts** of the surrounding communities allows teachers to better understand flags for referrals. Teachers that continually assess their awareness of the cultures and diversity of the communities where they teach demonstrate cultural competence. In order for schools and teachers to be described as culturally competent, they should have a process for recognizing diversity. They should also learn about and incorporate knowledge of cultural diversity into their classrooms.

Cultural and Linguistic Differences vs. Learning Difficulties

Many schools are enriched with cultural diversity. It is important for special educators to identify if a suspected learning disability may instead be a **cultural or linguistic difference** in a student. Teachers and schools must increase awareness of cultural and linguistic differences in order to avoid overidentification of this population as having learning difficulties. Some ways a child's behavior may represent cultural or linguistic differences are demonstrated in the **interactions** between teachers and students. In some cultures, children are asked to make eye contact to ensure they are listening, whereas in other cultures, children are taught to look down or away when being spoken to by an adult. Certain facial expressions and behaviors may be interpreted differently by students due to their cultural backgrounds. Additionally, teaching methods that are comfortable and effective for some students may be ineffective for others due to differing cultural backgrounds. Cultural values and characteristics may vary between teachers and students and contribute to the students' school performances. It is important for teachers to be **self-aware** and constantly **assess** whether ineffective teaching methods are due to learning difficulties or differences in cultural and linguistic diversity.

Instructional Strategies for Teaching ESL Students and Students with Disabilities

English as a Second Language (ESL) students are often at risk for being **referred** for special education services. This is frequently a result of **inadequate planning** for the needs of English language learners rather than skill deficits. To ensure that the needs of ESL students are met and discrimination is avoided, educators can implement strategies for **targeting their learning processes**. Strategies similar to those utilized in inclusive special education settings are helpful, such as using visuals to supplement instruction. This type of nonlinguistic representation helps convey meaning to ESL students. Working in groups with peers helps students with disabilities and ESL students demonstrate communication and social skills while working toward common goals. Allowing students to write and speak in their first languages until they feel comfortable speaking in English is a scaffolding strategy that can also be implemented. Sentence frames that demonstrate familiar sentence formats are helpful for all students to practice speaking and writing in structured, formal ways.

Teaching Appropriate Communication Skills

Students with disabilities who are also English Language Learners (ELLs) have the additional challenge of **language barriers** affecting their access to learning. These barriers, combined with the disabilities, can also make instruction for these students challenging. For ELL students with disabilities, it is important for teachers to rely on **appropriate instructional strategies** in order to determine what is affecting the students' access to information. Instructional strategies for teaching ELL students are similar to teaching strategies used for nonverbal students. Pairing **visuals** with words helps students make concrete connections between the written words and the pictures. The consistency of seeing the words paired with the visuals increases the likelihood of the students beginning to interpret word meanings. Using **sign language** is another way teachers can facilitate word meaning. When used consistently, students make connections between the visual word meanings and the written words. Teachers can also provide opportunities for ELL students to access language by having all classroom students communicate in a **consistent manner**. The goal of this instructional strategy is for peers to model appropriate verbal communication as it applies to different classroom situations.

Benefits the Socratic Method

With the Socratic method of teaching, students are **guided** by their teachers in their own educational discovery learning processes. This involves students intrinsically seeking knowledge or answers to problems. This method can be helpful for facilitating and enhancing the **social and emotional abilities** of students with disabilities, particularly Autism Spectrum Disorder (ASD). The Socratic method requires **dialogue** in order to successfully facilitate the teacher/student guided learning process. This is beneficial for students with autism who generally struggle with appropriate communication and social skills. This method emphasizes **information seeking and communication skills** by engaging students in class discussions, assignment sharing, and group work. Communication for information-seeking purposes is often a deficit of students with ASD. Sharing of ideas is a concept that develops naturally in guided learning and often requires flexibility in the thought process, another skill that students with ASD struggle with. These skills can be taught and reinforced to students with and without disabilities in order to develop skills essential to life-long learning processes.

Erikson's Four Earliest Social Stages of Human Development

The stages of human development and behavior are separated into seven human age groups, with the four earliest being **infancy** (birth to 2 years old), **early childhood** (3 to 8 years old), **middle childhood** (9 to 11 years old), and **adolescence** (12 to 18 years old). As children age, they build upon each stage. Growth is unique to each individual. According to Erikson's theory of psychosocial development, each developmental stage is characterized by **crises**. During infancy, babies learn **trust versus mistrust (hope)**. This is when a nurtured and loved infant would develop trust, and a mistreated infant would not. The infancy stage is also formed by **autonomy versus shame (will)**. This stage is characterized by the exertion of will and the seeking of independence by small children. Early childhood is characterized by **learning initiative versus guilt (purpose)**. During this stage, children begin to develop their interpersonal skills. **Industry versus inferiority (competence)** also develops during early childhood. During this stage, teachers begin to play an important role, as school-aged children learn competence in new skills. Throughout middle childhood and adolescence, children learn **identity versus role confusion (fidelity)**. The identity stage is when adolescents seek to form their individual identities.

Values of the Social Cognitive Theory

The three values or valuables of the social cognitive theory are **behavioral factors, personal factors** (intrinsic), and **environmental factors** (extrinsic). The social cognitive behavior theory suggests that these three variables are connected to each other and therefore promote learning. The basic concepts of the social cognitive theory can become evident in infancy, childhood, and adulthood. These concepts include observational learning, reproduction, self-efficacy, emotional coping, and self-regulatory capability. **Observational learning** is the process by which people learn behavior by observing other behaviors. This is especially influenced by a person's environment. Reproduction occurs when a person repeats modeled behavior. **Reproduction** can be impeded by a person's limited abilities. **Self-efficacy** is when a person puts new knowledge or behavior into action. **Emotional coping** is a learning process where people develop coping skills for dealing with stressful environments and negative influences. The development of good emotional coping skills influences learning processes. **Self-regulatory capability** describes a person's ability to manage choices and behavior even when influenced by negative environments.

Gardner's Theory of Multiple Intelligences

Howard Gardner developed the theory of multiple intelligences, which outlines seven different ways he believes people can learn. Gardner's theory was based on the idea that everyone understands the world through different intelligences, and our **individual intelligence strengths** are what make people different. The multiple intelligences are described below.

- **Visual-spatial thinkers** think about things visually. They are very aware of their environments. They are good at activities like completing puzzles, drawing, and reading maps. They learn best through the use of visuals, such as graphs and diagrams.
- **Bodily-kinesthetic thinkers** learn best with a hands-on approach. They process information by doing. They learn best through physical activities.
- **Musical thinkers** are sensitive to music, sound, and rhythm in their environments. They learn best when lesson concepts are turned into musical features like lyrics and songs.
- **Interpersonal thinkers** like to learn by interacting with others. They find learning easy in group environments like seminars and lecture halls.
- **Intrapersonal thinkers** are independent learners. They learn best using introspection.
- **Linguistic thinkers** are efficient and use words to express themselves. They are auditory learners who enjoy reading, word games, and making up stories.
- **Logical-mathematical thinkers** learn best through familiar patterns and relationships. They think conceptually and reasonably.

Cognitive Behavioral Theory

The cognitive behavioral theory states that people form their own negative or positive concepts that affect their behaviors. The cognitive behavioral theory involves a **cognitive triad** of human thoughts and behaviors. This triad refers to human thoughts about the **self**, the **world and environment**, and the **future**. In times of stress, people's thoughts can become distressed or dysfunctional. Sometimes cognitive behavioral therapy, based on the cognitive behavioral theory model, is used to help people address and manage their thoughts. This process involves people examining their thoughts more closely in order to bring them back to more realistic, grounded ways of thinking. People's thoughts and perceptions can often affect their lives negatively and lead to unhealthy emotions and behaviors. **Cognitive behavioral therapy** helps people to adjust their thinking, learn ways to access healthy thoughts, and learn behaviors incompatible with unhealthy or unsafe behaviors.

Social and Emotional Skill Expectations and Milestones of Toddlers and Preschoolers

Toddlers **18 months to 2 years old** typically begin to demonstrate their **independence** and show an increasing interest in **communication**. Toddlers exhibit temper tantrums and an increase in defiant behavior. Children in this age group begin to **imitate** the actions of familiar adults and engage in pretend play. They also demonstrate an interest in playing with other children but engage in **side-by-side play** (parallel play) instead of cooperative play. Preschoolers ages **3 and 4** continue to demonstrate independence and build on their communication skills. They may also demonstrate temper tantrums and defiant behavior. Preschoolers are able to verbalize a wider range of **emotions**, especially when they do not get what they want or have trouble communicating what they want. They begin to engage with their peers in **cooperative play** and start to play independently. Preschoolers are still interested in and engage in pretend play. At this age, they begin to recognize adults' moods or feelings. They begin to exhibit moments of helpfulness and kindness.

Social and Emotional Skill Expectations and Milestones of Grade Schoolers

Children typically enter kindergarten at ages **5 to 6**. They begin to exert their **independence** and test **boundaries** at home and school. They show a preference to playing with kids their own ages and sometimes their own genders. Their conversational language grows as they interact with other students. At ages **7 to 8**, children start to become aware of what others might think of them. They may be more sensitive to **interpersonal relationships** with their peers. They can aptly express their feelings but get frustrated when they do not have the right words. At ages **9–10**, children begin getting selective with their **peer friendships**. They may prefer a few close friends over getting along with everyone. They begin to demonstrate more **independence** and start attempting to develop their own **identities**. Children in this age group are able to communicate their feelings but can still get frustrated. They demonstrate a wide range of emotions in adult and peer interactions.

Piaget's Four Stages of Cognitive Development

Piaget's four stages of cognitive development are sensorimotor (birth to 18 months), preoperational (18-24 months to age 7), concrete operational (ages 7 to 12), and formal operational (adolescence to adulthood). During the **sensorimotor stage**, newborn infants only have a minute awareness. As they grow, they begin to interact with their environments before developing object permanence at 7–9 months. Another important milestone that develops during this stage is early language development. During the **preoperational stage**, infants grow into young children and their language becomes more meaningful. They develop memory and imagination but cannot yet grasp complex concepts such as cause and effect. The **concrete operational stage** is characterized by concrete reasoning. Children in this stage become more aware of the world around them and are less egocentric. They cannot yet think abstractly or hypothetically. During the **formal operational stage**, adolescents are able to engage in abstract thinking. They are now able to formulate hypotheses and demonstrate logical thought and deductive reasoning.

Rights and the Roles Families in the Educations of Children with Disabilities

Under IDEA, parents and legal guardians of children with disabilities have **procedural safeguards** that protect their rights. The safeguards also provide parents and legal guardians of children with disabilities with the means to resolve any disputes with school systems. Families serve as **advocates** for their children with disabilities. **Parents and legal guardians** may underestimate their importance to Individualized Education Program teams. However, they are important members of the Individualized Education Program teams and integral parts of the decision-making processes for their children's educational journeys. Parents and legal guardians often work more closely with their children than other adults. Therefore, as part of the IEP teams, parents and legal guardians often provide insight regarding the children's backgrounds, educational histories, developmental histories, strengths, and weaknesses. Parents and legal guardians are also important decision makers in transition meetings, when students with disabilities move from one level of school to another. Parent and legal guardian input in transition meetings ensures that appropriate services and supports are in place within the next levels of school in order to ensure student success.

Assessment and Evaluation

Types of Developmental Assessments

Developmental assessments measure the development of infants, toddlers, and preschoolers. These **norm-referenced tests** measure fine and gross motor skills, communication and language, and social, cognitive, and self-help milestones that young children should achieve at certain ages. When a child is suspected of having a **developmental delay**, a developmental assessment is useful in identifying the child's strengths and weaknesses. Developmental assessments map out the **progress** of a child compared to the progress of similar-aged children. Developmental assessments are also useful in identifying if the delay is significant or can be overcome with time. These assessments can be used to determine what **educational placement** is most appropriate for a child with a developmental delay. Developmental assessments are administered via observations and questionnaires. Parents, legal guardians, caregivers, and instructors who are most familiar with the child provide the most insight on developmental strengths and weaknesses.

Screening Tests for Identifying Students

When determining if a child needs special education, **screening tests** are the first step. The Individuals with Disabilities Education Act (IDEA) offers guidance for schools to implement screening tests. Districts and schools often have school-wide processes in place for screening students for **special education**. Screening tests can also be used to identify students who are falling behind in class. The advantage of screening tests is that they are easily administered. They require few materials and little time and planning in order to administer. Additionally, they can be used to quickly assess students' strengths and weaknesses. They do not have to be administered one-on-one and can be used class wide. Screening tests can be as simple as paper and pencil quizzes assessing what students know. Screening tests are used for measuring visual acuity, auditory skills, physical health, development, basic academic skills, behavioral problems, children at risk for behavioral problems, language skills, and verbal and nonverbal intelligence.

Individual Intelligence Tests vs. Individual Academic Achievement Tests

Intelligence tests measure a student's capacity for abstract thinking, mental reasoning, judgment, and decision-making. These **norm-referenced tests** help determine a student's **overall intelligence**, which correlates with **potential academic performance**. Intelligence tests can be used to determine if a student's deficits are due to intellectual disabilities or related to specific learning disabilities or emotional disorders. Intelligence tests are also known as **intelligence quotient tests (IQ tests)**. IQ tests should be administered by trained professionals in order to ensure the tests are administered accurately. Intelligence tests can also measure verbal skills, motor performance, and visual reasoning. Unlike intelligence tests, individual academic tests measure a student's strengths and weaknesses in individual skills. They are also norm referenced and used to determine if a student needs **special education services**. Results from individual academic tests help determine areas of concern or possible deficits for an individual student. Unlike intelligence tests, individual academic tests can be administered by teachers.

Adaptive Behavior Scale Assessments

Adaptive behavior scales are useful for diagnosing a student with an **intellectual disability** that affects the development or progression of adaptive behavior. They are used in preschools and for determining eligibility for **special education** in grade schools. They are also used in planning

43

curriculum for students with intellectual disabilities. Adaptive behavior scales are standardized but not always norm referenced because of difficulties comparing expectations for some adaptive and maladaptive skills exhibited by similar-aged peers. In terms of curriculum planning, these assessments can determine what type and how much assistance a student may need. Adaptive behavior scale assessments identify a student's level of **independence**. Adaptive behavior scales can be used to determine **skill abilities** associated with daily living, community functioning, social skills, communication, motor functions, and basic academic skills. Teachers and other professionals can administer adaptive behavior scales to students with intellectual disabilities to determine starting points for improving their adaptive behavior deficits.

Curriculum Based Measurement for Measuring Student Academic Progress

Curriculum Based Measurement (**CBM**) is a way for teachers to track how students are **progressing** in mathematics, language arts, social studies, science, and other skills. CBM is useful for addressing how students with special needs are progressing on their Individualized Education Program (IEP) goals. It is also useful for communicating progress to parents or legal guardians. CBM results can determine whether or not current **instructional strategies** are effective for particular students. In the same respect, CBM can determine if students are meeting the **standards** laid out in their IEP goals. If instructional strategies are not effective or their goals are not being met, CBM progress (or lack of progress) signals that the teachers should change instructional strategies. CBM can be revisited to determine whether or not the newly implemented strategies are effective. Progress can sometimes be charted to present a visual for how a student is progressing in a particular content area or with a specific skill.

Woodcock Johnson Achievement Tests

High-Incidence Disabilities

Woodcock Johnson achievement tests can be used as diagnostic tools for identifying children with **high-incidence disabilities**. The Woodcock Johnson Tests of Achievement and the Woodcock Johnson Tests of Cognitive Abilities are comprehensively useful for assessing children's:

- intellectual abilities.
- cognitive abilities.
- aptitude.
- oral language.
- academic achievements.

These norm-referenced tests are valuable in understanding children's strengths and weaknesses and how they compare to cohorts of normally progressing, similar-aged peers. For example, Woodcock Johnson Tests (**WJ tests**) are useful in identifying children with language disorders because children with language disorders typically score lower on the Listening Comprehension and Fluid Reasoning test sections. The WJ tests are useful diagnostic tools for identifying children with Attention Deficit Hyperactivity Disorder (ADHD) as well. While children with ADHD may perform similarly to children with learning disabilities, their key deficits are in the Cognitive Efficiency, Processing Speed, Academic Fluency, Short-Term Memory, and Long-Term Retrieval test sections.

Learning Disabilities in Reading and Mathematics

The Woodcock Johnson achievement tests (**WJ tests**) include a test of **achievement** and a test of **cognitive abilities**. Together, these assessments are useful in the diagnostic process of identifying a student with a **disability**. Additionally, they are helpful for identifying specific **deficits** in a student's reading or math skills. WJ tests are norm referenced and compare the results of a child's performance to that of a cohort of children of similar chronological age and average intellectual abilities. These assessments provide information about a child's **reading disorder**, such as dyslexia, because they measure phonological awareness, rapid automatized naming, processing speed, and working memory. WJ tests report on a child's cognitive functioning in these test areas. These assessments also provide useful information for students with learning deficits in **mathematics**. Performances on the Math Calculation Skills and Math Reasoning test sections provide information on specific deficits in general comprehension, fluid reasoning, and processing speed. Children that have deficits in these areas demonstrate relationships to learning disabilities in mathematics.

Evaluating Students with Special Needs Using the Weschler Intelligence Scale

The Weschler Intelligence Scale is an assessment that measures the cognitive abilities of children and adults. The **Weschler Intelligence Scale for Children (WISC)** measures a child's **verbal intelligence** (including comprehension and vocabulary) and **performance intelligence** (including reasoning and picture completion). The WISC is an intelligence quotient test that is useful for helping diagnose a student with a **cognitive disability**. A score below 100 indicates below-average intelligence. WISC results are useful tools for evaluating a student with a disability. Tests results can be used to measure and report on a student's general intelligence and provide insight into the student's cognitive abilities in order to determine an appropriate educational pathway. Results can be reported in a student's Evaluation Team Report and Individualized Education Program in order to justify special education services or have a starting point for Individualized Education Program goals. WISC results are especially important in an Evaluation Team Report, generally completed every 3 years or less, because they contribute to describing the **overall performance profile** of a student with a disability.

Kaufman Assessment Battery for Children

The Kaufman Assessment Battery for Children (**K-ABC**) is a unique standardized test because it is used to evaluate preschoolers, minority groups, and children with learning disabilities. The K-ABC can be used to assess children ages 2–18 and is meant to be used with children who are nonverbal, bilingual, or English speaking. However, it is especially useful in assessing the abilities of students who are **nonverbal**. The K-ABC can be used to help determine students' educational placements and assist with their educational planning. This assessment has four components that measure students' abilities, which are described below.

- The **sequential processing scale** assesses short-term memory and problem-solving skills when putting things in sequential order.
- The **simultaneous processing scale** assesses problem-solving skills for completing multiple processes simultaneously, such as identifying objects and reproducing design shapes using manipulatives.
- The **achievement component** measures expressive vocabulary, mathematics skills, and reading and decoding skills.
- The **mental processing component** assesses the abilities a student demonstrates on the sequential and simultaneous processing scales.

The K-ABC is also unique because it includes a **nonverbal scale** that can be administered to children with hearing or speech impairments and children who do not speak English.

Vineland Adaptive Behavior Scale

The Vineland Adaptive Behavior Scale (**VABS**) assesses the personal and social skills of children and adults. **Adaptive behavior** refers to the skills needed for day-to-day activities and independent living. Children with disabilities sometimes have deficits in adaptive behavior, and the VABS is useful for planning their **educational pathways**. It is an especially useful tool for developing **transition plans and goals** for students of appropriate ages on Individualized Education Programs. The VABS is a process that involves people who know the students best, like parents and/or teachers. The teacher version and parent version of this assessment can be delivered via interview or survey. The parent version focuses on a student's adaptive behavior at home, while the teacher version focuses on adaptive behavior in the school setting. Version II of the VABS assesses four **domains**: communication, daily living skills, socialization, and social skills. A student's comprehensive score from both the teacher and parent version are used to report abilities in the four domains.

Types of Cognitive Assessments

Cognitive tests assess the **cognitive functioning abilities** of children and adults. They are useful tools for diagnosing and/or identifying children with disabilities who are eligible for **special education services** under the Individuals with Disabilities Education Act. Examples of cognitive tests used in diagnosing or identifying children with disabilities include aptitude tests and intelligence quotient (IQ) tests. There are also cognitive assessments that measure verbal reasoning, numerical reasoning, abstract reasoning, spatial ability, verbal ability, and more. Children's cognitive abilities are related to how quickly they **process** information. Assessment results can be good measurements of how quickly children may learn new information or tasks. Cognitive assessments provide specific information about children's cognitive functioning by providing measurements of their intelligence, attention, concentration, processing speed, language and communication, visual-spatial abilities, and short and long-term memory capabilities. Individual assessment results can be used to evaluate a child's need for special education services. Results can also be used on a child's Evaluation Team Report or for developing goals on the Individualized Education Program.

Prenatal, Perinatal, and Neonatal Disabilities

Prenatal, perinatal, and neonatal risk factors can be genetic or environmental. These risk factors put infants at risk for developing **intellectual disabilities** that affect their day-to-day lives. An intellectual disability (**ID**) is a disability that significantly limits a child's overall cognitive abilities. **Prenatal risk factors** include genetic syndromes (i.e. Down Syndrome), brain malformation, maternal diseases, and environmental influences. Drugs, alcohol, or poison exposure can all affect an unborn child. **Perinatal (during delivery) risk factors** include labor and delivery trauma or anoxia at birth. **Neonatal (post-birth) risk factors** include hypoxic ischemic injury (brain injury), traumatic brain injury, infections, seizure disorders, and toxic metabolic syndromes. Early screening and applicable assessments are tools used to identify young children with intellectual disabilities. Early screening and assessments can assist with providing a child with ID with special education services under the Individuals with Disabilities Education Act. These tools can also help assess the severity of need, deficit areas, and need for special services, such as occupational therapy.

Advantages and Disadvantages of Curriculum-Based Assessments

Curriculum-based assessments (**CBAs**) are assessments that determine if students are making adequate progress through the curriculum. They can be administered by a teacher, special educator, or school psychologist. CBAs have advantages over norm-referenced assessments, like developmental assessments, because they are not used to compare performances between students. Other types of assessments measure a student's cumulative abilities across multiple skills instead of assessing individual skills. CBAs measure student progress in more **individualized** ways. They are especially useful for measuring Individualized Education Program (IEP) goal progress. Since CBAs are **teacher-created assessments**, they provide opportunities to assess students informally and formally on IEP goals. For example, a teacher may verbally quiz a student on ten addition problems to determine if the student is making progress on math IEP goals. CBAs are also used in the Response to Intervention process to identify students with special needs by measuring the effectiveness of interventions provided to them.

Advantages and Disadvantages of Using Formal Assessments

Formal assessments measure whether or not students are learning what they are supposed to be learning. Formal assessments help teachers determine what their students know. They typically measure how students are **performing** compared to their similar-aged peers. Examples of formal assessments include quizzes, tests, standardized tests, achievement tests, aptitude tests, and norm-referenced tests.

Formal assessments have the same set of expectations for all students and are graded using the same criteria. However, students with disabilities do not always learn or retain previously taught content in the same ways as their similar-aged peers. Using **universal criteria** to assess what students have learned is one disadvantage to formal assessments for students with disabilities. An advantage of formal assessments is that they allow teachers to collect **baseline data** on students' educational performances by comparing their performances to age or grade-based performance criteria. Additionally, students with disabilities can receive **accommodations and modifications** on these types of assessments. Accommodations and modifications are implemented based on needs specific to each student. The goal is to level the playing field for these students on formal assessments, like standardized state tests.

Uses, Advantages, and Disadvantages of Using Informal Assessments

Informal assessments can provide teachers with a lot of information about students' educational **strengths and weaknesses**. Informal assessments are also used to guide teachers' daily instruction by providing constant and immediate **feedback** about students' learning processes. Examples of informal assessments include observations and rating scales, checks of daily work, homework, group projects, checklists, and rubrics.

Informal assessments offer some advantages. They are often easy to implement and allow teachers to gather useful data. Informal assessments may naturally be less stressful for students because they do not realize they are being tested. When test stress factors are removed, results from informal assessments may provide the best reflections of students' **abilities**.

Disadvantages of informal assessments include **hidden bias or stereotypes** within the person administering the assessment. Teachers implementing informal assessments must be conscious of and avoid bias in order to receive accurate information about students' educational performances. Another disadvantage is that students may also feel more pressure to perform well on formal

47

assessments versus informal assessments, affecting their performances on the informal assessments.

How Formative Assessments Work

The goals of formative assessments are to provide ongoing feedback and monitor students' learning. These assessments are a process of informal assessment strategies that help educators gather information about student learning. Formative assessments help **differentiate instruction** and are considered part of the **student learning process**. Formative assessments communicate what the students are learning and also check for understanding. They provide information needed to adjust teaching and learning while it is happening.

Formative assessments also provide opportunities for students to receive **feedback** on their individual performances and engage in their paths to success. Teachers can use formative assessments to allow students to participate in the learning process, outside of sitting and listening to lectures. **Discussions** are examples of formative assessments, where teachers can initiate discussions about topics and gauge students' understanding. **Exit slips** are written questions posed by teachers at the ends of their classes, intended to determine what the students have learned. The **think, pair, share method** requires students to work together to solve problems. Students are asked to brainstorm answers to questions posed by the teachers, then they are paired with other students before sharing their thinking with their partners.

How Summative Assessments Work

Summative assessments are less flexible than formative assessments due to how performance data is collected. The goal of summative assessment is to evaluate what a student has learned at the **end of an instructional section or unit**. Summative assessments often measure the mastery of learning standards.

Summative assessments use standards or benchmarks to measure student success at certain **checkpoints** during the learning process. They are almost always high stakes, heavily weighted (unlike formative assessments), and formally graded. Information from summative assessments can be used to report on student progress. Teachers can use a variety of summative assessments to determine where students are in the learning process. These types of assessments also play a role in identifying benchmarked progress and the educational needs of students with disabilities.

These types of assessments feature a narrower range of question types, such as multiple choice, short answer, and essay questions. Examples of summative assessments include state tests, end of unit or chapter tests, end of semester exams, and assessments that formally measure the mastery of a particular benchmark.

Alternate Assessments

Students with and without disabilities are typically expected to take the same standardized tests, sometimes with accommodations and/or modifications. Some students with disabilities take **alternate assessments**, which are forms of the standardized tests that other students take. Students that participate in alternate assessments are unable to participate in state standardized tests even with accommodations. Less than 1% of students in public school districts participate in alternate assessments. They are mostly intended for students with **intellectual disabilities** or **severe cognitive delays**. Alternate assessments are based on **Alternate Achievement Standards (AAS)**, which are modified versions of state achievement standards. Alternate assessments are a way for students' progress to be assessed with standards that are more appropriate for their skills.

Teachers, parents, and students work collaboratively to demonstrate that the achievement standards are met. For example, a state standard for math may not be appropriate for a student with an intellectual disability. Instead, the student may have the alternative standard of demonstrating the ability to count money to make a purchase.

Role Formal Assessments Play in the Education of a Student with Disabilities

Formal assessments measure how well a student has mastered learning material and are useful in detecting if a student is **falling behind** in general or at the end of a taught unit. Formal test results can be used to compare the performance of a student with disabilities against other students of similar demographics. **Developmental assessments** are norm-referenced tests that are designed to assess the development of small children. Developmental assessments are used to identify the strengths and weaknesses of a child suspected of having a disability. **Intelligence tests** are another type of norm-referenced test that can determine a student's potential to learn academic skills. Intelligence tests, sometimes called IQ tests, also indicate a student's specific level of intelligence. This is helpful in knowing if a student's learning problems are associated with sub-average intellectual abilities or other factors, such as an emotional disturbance. A student with an emotional disturbance or specific learning disability would have an average or above-average intelligence score, whereas a student with intellectual disabilities would have a sub-average score. **Curriculum-based assessments** are also helpful in determining where, specifically, a student needs the most help within a content area.

Interest Inventories

Interest inventories are tools for measuring people's interests or preferences in activities. They are useful for gathering information about a student's likes and dislikes. In special education, interest inventories are sometimes used to help develop the **transition portion** of an Individualized Education Plan (IEP). A student's interests as determined by an interest inventory can be used to drive the entire IEP. For an older student with a driving interest in mind, interest inventories can also be reflected in the annual IEP goals. Interest inventories can come in the form of observations, ability tests, or self-reporting inventories. They can also work as age-appropriate **transition assessments** used in the transition statement section of the IEP. An advantage of interest inventories is they help students get to know their strengths and interests. They are also useful in guiding students with disabilities into thinking about post-secondary careers, education, or independent living.

Role Informal Assessments Play in the Education of a Student with Disabilities

Informal assessments are a little more flexible for teachers, particularly in the ways they can be administered in the classroom. In special education, informal assessments play an important role in **adjusting instruction** to meet the specific needs of the student. Using informal assessment outcomes to drive instruction ensures that academic or behavioral student needs are met. Informal assessments are also helpful in adjusting instruction to meet **specific goals or objectives** on a student's Individualized Education Program. Checklists, running records, observations, and work samples are all informal assessments from which data for IEP goals can be collected. **Checklists** can include a list of behaviors or academic skills the student is meant to achieve. Checklists enable the teacher to check off skills that a student can do. **Running records** help provide insight into student behavior over time by focusing on a sequence of events. **Work samples** are helpful in providing a concrete snapshot of a student's academic capabilities.

Developing and Writing Measurable IEP Goals

According to the Individuals with Disabilities Education Act (IDEA), Individualized Education Program goals must contain specific **components** for students eligible for special education and placed on IEPs. Components of a **measurable IEP goal** include condition, performance, criteria, assessment, and standard. **Condition** refers to when, where, and how the disability will be addressed. For example, an IEP goal may state, "By the end of this IEP, Jacob will use appropriate skills to communicate his needs in 4/5 trials." "By the end of this IEP" is the condition of the goal. **Performance** is what the student is expected to accomplish during the condition of the goal. "Jacob will use appropriate skills to communicate his needs" is a performance example in the goal above. The last part of the goal stating "in 4/5 trials" is the **criteria** that outlines how well the goal will be performed. Measurable goals also include how skill mastery will be **assessed**, such as through observations or work samples. Goals should also be **standards-based**, and goals must be connected to state standards.

Determining the Placement of a Student with a Disability

With every student, the goal is placement in the **general education classroom** as much as possible, while still meeting the student's educational needs and ensuring a successful educational experience. IDEA does not require that students be placed in the regular education classroom. However, this is the first option that should be considered by a student's IEP team. Ultimately, the IEP determines what **environment** best suits the student based on the student's specific needs. The IEP is responsible for determining what educational environment would provide the student with the maximum appropriate educational benefit. While justification for removing a student from the regular education classroom is common and appropriate, as occurs when a student is placed in a resource room, the IEP team must explain the reasoning on the student's IEP. **Justification** must specifically list why the student cannot be educated with accommodations and services in the regular education classroom during any part of the school day. Justification for removal cannot be due to perceived instructional limitations of the regular education teacher or concerns over extra instructional time needed to educate a student with a disability.

Roles/Responsibilities of the Special Education Instructor in Full/Partial Inclusion Setting vs. a Self-Contained Classroom

Students with mild to moderate disabilities are often placed in **inclusion** or **partial inclusion classrooms**. The responsibilities of the special educator include assisting and collaborating with the general education teacher to create a curriculum with **modifications** that meets the learning styles and needs of the students with disabilities. The special educator may circulate during lessons or classwork to help students when needed and provide modifications to the general education curriculum to best meet the individual needs of each student.

The role of a special educator in a **self-contained classroom** is much different. Students in a self-contained classroom typically have disabilities that severely limit their abilities to receive quality education in inclusion or partial inclusion settings. Students with moderate disabilities in self-contained classrooms receive **modified instruction** with accommodations. The special educator is usually assisted by teaching assistants or paraprofessionals who help the educator meet the needs of individual students.

Special educators in inclusion, partial inclusion, and self-contained classrooms share some similar **responsibilities**. These responsibilities include monitoring IEP data on annual goals for each student, giving standardized pretests and posttests, facilitating parent-teacher conferences, completing annual IEP reviews, and developing curriculum.

Specially Designed Instruction

Specially Designed Instruction (**SDI**) in special education refers to the teaching methods and strategies used by special educators to teach students with learning disabilities and other learning disorders. SDI is used to meet the specific needs of learners who may not be successful learning in the same ways as their similar-aged peers. SDI should be adapted to the **unique learning needs** of students, address the learning issues specific to a child's disability, and ensure student access to the general education classroom. In SDI, the teaching methodology should be changed without sacrificing content aligned with the state standards.

Universal Design for Learning

The universal design for learning is a flexible approach to learning that keeps students' individual needs in mind. Teachers that utilize **UDL** offer different ways for students to access material and engage in content. This approach is helpful for many students, but particularly those with learning and attention issues. The three main principles of UDL are **representation**, **action and expression**, and **engagement**. Through these principles, UDL ensures multiple means of representation, multiple ways for students to interact with the material, and multiple ways to motivate students.

Role of Local Education Agency Members in the IEP Meetings

Local education agency (**LEA**) representatives represent local educational agencies and are knowledgeable about special education curriculum, general education curriculum, and community resources. An LEA member is also referred to as a **district representative**. An LEA member is a member of the school district where any special education meetings take place. In an **Individualized Education Program (IEP) meeting**, LEAs are members of the school district that referred the student for special education services. LEAs contribute their knowledge during the IEP meeting. An LEA member must be a licensed professional who knows the student and is familiar with the IEP process. The role of LEA members in IEP meetings is to make sure the information presented is compliant with the Individuals with Disabilities Education Act (IDEA) standards. LEAs are also responsible for ensuring that the school district is **compliant** with procedural components of IDEA and that eligible students are receiving free and appropriate public educations (FAPEs).

Involvement of Students on IEPs in the Transition Process in High School

Most states require **transition statements** to be made when students reach age 14 during the Individualized Education Program (IEP) year. Federal law requires students 16 years of age or older to have transition statements, post-secondary goals for independent living, employment, and education, and summaries of performance that include the results of the most recent transition assessments. Per federal law, students of transition age must be invited to their **IEP meetings**. It is important for students on IEPs to **participate** in the transition process because it helps them figure out what they want to do after they graduate from high school. Participation in the process gets them thinking about living independently, post-secondary education options, and employment options. Students usually have opportunities to participate in formal and informal assessments like interest inventories that help them narrow their interests. Transition goals for independent living, employment, and education should be based on the results of these assessments and any other interests the students have expressed. The students participate in the **implementation** of the transition goals by completing activities associated with their indicated interests.

Role of the Support Team in the Education of a Child with a Disability

A **student support team (SST)** assists with identifying and supporting a student needing special education services. In this support team model, a group of educators works to identify and provide early intervention services for any student exhibiting academic or behavioral problems. Most schools have a system by which the interventions for the student are implemented. The purpose of this SST is to offer different supports, such as monitoring student progress, developing intervention plans, and referring students for intervention services. While the primary goal of this SST is to provide support for students **struggling with school**, it can also shift focus to supporting students at risk of **dropping out of school**.

A support team can also be a team of **professionals** in charge of the implementation of an IEP for a student with a disability. A student-based support team is created for any student with an IEP. The purpose of this SST is to enhance a student's learning process and development. Members of this type of SST include the child, parent or legal guardian, special educator, a general educator, and a representative of the school system. The SST may also include relevant service professionals, student or parent advocates, school psychologists, or any others with knowledge or expertise about the student.

Amendments to an Individualized Education Program

A student's Individualized Education Program **(IEP)** is in effect for one year. Academic goals, objectives, benchmarks, transition goals, and any accommodations and modifications are to be in place for the student for the duration of the IEP. An **amendment** can be made when a change needs to be made to the IEP before the year is over. An amendment is an agreement between the student, parents or legal guardians, and the IEP team. IEP meetings for amendments can be requested at any time. IEP amendments can be requested if a student is not making adequate progress toward the goals, if the goals become inappropriate in some way for the student, or when the student has met all IEP goals and requires new ones. If new information about the student becomes available, the IEP can be amended. Students who need accommodations and modifications added or removed can also request amendment meetings.

How Needs of Students with IEPs Are Met in the School Environment

IEPs communicate what **services** are to be provided for children with disabilities in the school setting, the children's **present levels of performance (PLOPs)**, and how their disabilities affect **academic performance**. IEPs also specify **annual goals** appropriate to the students' specific needs and any accommodations or modifications that need to be provided. Schools and teachers working with students with disabilities have the responsibility to implement these IEP components when working with the students. Additionally, schools and teachers working with students with disabilities must ensure that the students' individualized annual goals are met within a year of the students' IEP effective dates. It is up to the IEP teams to determine what classroom settings would most benefit the students, while also appropriately meeting their IEP goals with the fewest barriers. Special educators must determine how data is collected, then record and obtain data on how the students are meeting their IEP goals. Special educators are responsible for providing intervention services based on the data results. They must also ensure that any accommodations or modifications listed on the IEPs are implemented in both general education and self-contained classrooms.

Accommodation Vs. Modification in IEPs

Formal accommodations and modifications for a student with a disability are listed on the Individualized Education Program. **Accommodations** change *how* a student learns the material, while a **modification** changes *what* a student is taught or expected to learn. In classroom instruction, accommodations level the playing field for students with disabilities by helping them learn the same material and have the same expectations as their classmates. For example, a student with a reading difficulty might receive the accommodation of being able to listen to the text being read. Modifications are for students who are academically far behind their peers. An example of a classroom instructional modification would be a student receiving a shorter reading assignment or an assignment catered to the student's reading level.

Accommodations for tests look a little different because the tests are assessing what the students learned. An appropriate example of a **test accommodation** is giving the student extra time to complete the test. **Classroom test modifications** may involve giving the students less to learn and including less material on the tests. For state standardized tests, accommodations like extra time and frequent breaks can be provided. Students that need modifications to state tests may complete alternate assessments that may not cover the same material as the standard exams.

Ensuring a SMART Annual Goal in an IEP

A good IEP goal describes how far the student is expected to **progress** toward the IEP goal by the next IEP. Since IEPs should be revised once a year, a good annual IEP goal should describe what the student is capable of doing in a one-year time frame. Creating **SMART** IEP goals can help the student determine realistic expectations for what can be achieved in a year. SMART IEP goals are specific, measurable, attainable, results oriented, and timebound. Goals are **specific** when they list the targeted result of the skill or subject area. Goals should also be specific to the student's needs. Goals that are **measurable** state the way a student's progress will be measured. Measurable goals list how accurately a student should meet the goal. **Attainable** goals mean the goal is realistic for the student to achieve in one year. **Results-oriented** goals outline what a student needs to do to accomplish the goal. For example, a SMART goal may state, "During the school week, Robert will use his device to communicate greetings 80% of the time in 4/5 trials." **Time-bound** goals include a timeframe for the student to achieve the goal. They also list when and how often progress will be measured.

Role an Initial Evaluation Assessment Plays in Qualifying a Student for Special Education

When a student is determined to need special education, it means the student has a disability or disabilities adversely affecting educational performance. It may also mean the student's needs cannot be addressed in the general education classroom with or without accommodations, and **specially designed instruction (SDI)** is required. An **initial evaluation** of the student is required for special education eligibility. The evaluation is comprehensive and includes existing data collected on the student and additional assessments needed to determine eligibility. Individual school districts decide what assessments should be completed for the student's initial evaluation. Each district is responsible for and should provide assessments that measure functional, developmental, and academic information. The student's parents or legal guardians are responsible for providing outside information relevant to the student's education, such as medical needs assessed outside of the school district by qualified providers.

Purpose of an IEP for an Individual Student

The purpose of an Individualized Education Program is to guide the learning of a student with a **disability** in the educational environment. An Individualized Education Program is a written statement for a student eligible for **special education**. An initial IEP is **implemented** once the child has been evaluated and determined as needing special education. After the initial IEP, **IEP meetings** are conducted annually (or more) in order to update the plan to meet the needs of the student. IEPs are created, reviewed, and revised according to individual state and federal laws. These plans include the amount of time the student will spend in the special education classroom based on the level of need. They also include any related services the student might need, such as speech-language therapy, and academic and behavioral goals for the year. As the student learns and changes, performance levels and goals change as well. A student's present levels of performance are included and updated yearly, as are the academic and behavioral goals.

Members of an Individualized Education Program Team

Individualized Education Programs are conducted **annually**, following the initial IEP. IEP team members meet at least once a year to discuss a student's progress and make changes to the IEP. The required members of a student's IEP team include the student's parents or legal guardians, one of the student's general education teachers, the special education teacher, a school representative, an individual who can interpret the instructional implications of evaluation results, anyone else who has knowledge or expertise about the student, and, if appropriate, the student. **Parents and legal guardians** contribute unique expertise about the student, typically having the benefit of knowing the child well. **General education teachers** can speak on behalf of how the student is performing in the general education classroom. The **special education teacher** can report on progress made toward academic and behavioral goals and present levels of performance. A **school representative** must be qualified to provide or supervise specially designed instruction, be knowledgeable of the general education curriculum, and be knowledgeable about school resources. The **individual who can interpret evaluation results** can be an existing team member or someone else who is qualified to report on evaluation results. **Advocates**, such as counselors or therapists who see the student outside the school day, can also attend the meeting to speak on the student's behalf.

Legal Rights for Parents or Legal Guardians

Individualized Education Program (IEP) meetings occur annually for each student. However, it is a **parent or legal guardian's right** to request a meeting at any point during the school year. The student's school is responsible for identifying and evaluating the child, developing, reviewing, and/or revising the IEP, and determining what placement setting best suits the needs of the student. It is within the parent or legal guardian's rights to have **input** in all processes related to the student. Under the Individuals with Disabilities Education Act (IDEA), parents have the right to participate in IEP meetings, have an independent evaluation outside the one the school provides, give or deny consent for the IEP, contest a school's decision, and obtain private education paid for by the public school. In specific circumstances, if the student is determined to need services that the public school cannot provide, the public school district may need to pay for the student's tuition at a private school where the student's needs can be met.

Collaborative Consultation Between Educational Professionals

Collaborative consultation refers to the special educator or other professional providing advice to the general education teacher about the student on the Individualized Education Program. Special educators and other IEP team members, such as school psychologists and related service professionals, serve as the **experts** and have knowledge about how individual students learn and behave. This is especially important when students with IEPs are included in the general education classroom. Special educators and general education teachers must work collaboratively to ensure that students are reaching their potential in the general education setting. Examples of **collaborative consultation** include the special educator serving as a consultant to the general education teacher by providing advice on a student's IEP, accommodations, modifications, skill techniques, and IEP goal tracking. Another way the special educator or other professional can assist the general educator is by providing skill and strategy instruction to students on IEPs outside the general education classroom. The idea behind this method is for students to generalize these skills and strategies to the general education classroom.

Public School Responsibilities to Parents and Legal Guardians of Students on IEPs

The school must invite the parents or legal guardians to any **IEP meetings** and provide advance notice of the meetings. Each meeting notice is required to include the purpose of the meeting, its time and location, and who will attend. The location of the meeting is likely the student's school, but legally it must be held at a mutually agreed upon place and time. If the parent or legal guardian cannot attend the IEP meeting, the school must ensure participation in another way, such as video or telephone conference. The meeting can be conducted without the parent or legal guardian if the school district cannot get the parent or legal guardian to attend. A parent or legal guardian can request a meeting, and the school can refuse or deny the request. If denied, the school must provide a **Prior Written Notice** explaining their refusal. A Prior Written Notice is a document outlining important school district decisions about a student on an IEP.

Environmental Modifications for Students with Disabilities in the Classroom

Students with disabilities may need environmental modifications in order to be successful in their classrooms, homes, and communities. **Environmental modifications** are adaptations that allow people with disabilities to maneuver through their environments with as little resistance as possible. They allow for more **independent living experiences**, especially for those with limited mobility. Environmental modifications ensure the health, safety, and welfare of the people who need them. Examples of environmental modifications in the home, community, or school include ramps, hydraulic lifts, widened doorways and hallways, automatic doors, handrails, and grab bars. Roll-in showers, water faucet controls, worktable or work surface adaptations, and cabinet and shelving adaptations are also environmental modifications that can be provided if necessary. Other adaptations include heating and cooling adaptations and electrical adaptations to accommodate devices or equipment. Environmental modifications in the home are typically provided by qualified agencies or providers. The Americans with Disabilities Act ensures that environmental modifications are provided in the **community** to avoid the discrimination of a person with a disability.

Characteristics of Effective Structured Learning Environments

A structured learning environment is an important component of good **classroom management**. Teachers that create environments that are conducive for teaching and learning create environments where students feel safe. In **effective structured learning environments**, teachers create solid relationships with students by getting to know them and their interests. Often, this information can be used to implement learning activities based on students' interests. Another way to promote effective structured learning environments is to consistently follow implemented rules and maintain **consistency** in procedures in order to communicate what to expect to students. Transitioning students appropriately between activities increases time spent learning. Additionally, teachers that spend time designing effective lesson plans that anticipate student behaviors create solid environments for their students. Teachers can also establish good learning environments by promoting target behaviors. This means promoting standards of behavior and clear consequences for breaking rules. Students that have clear expectations learn in effective structured learning environments.

Curriculum and Assignment Modifications in the Classroom for Students with Disabilities

Modifications are changes to what students are taught or expected to learn. Students with disabilities can receive **curriculum modifications** as determined by their specific needs and as written out in their Individualized Education Programs. Curriculum modifications allow students to learn material that is different from what their general education peers learn. For example, students with classroom modifications may receive assignments with fewer math problems or with reading samples appropriate for their reading levels. Students with curriculum modifications may receive different grading tiers than their peers. The ways teachers grade their assignments may be different from how the teachers grade their peers' assignments. Students may also be excused from particular projects or given project guidelines that are different and better suited to their individual needs. **Assignment modifications** include completing fewer or different homework problems than peers, writing shorter papers, answering fewer questions on classwork and tests, and creating alternate projects or assignments.

Purpose of Non-Traditional Classroom Seating Arrangements

Seating arrangements are part of good classroom management strategies, especially for students with disabilities. Special education settings and inclusion settings often require flexibility with instruction and versatility with **seating arrangements**. The traditional setting includes rows of desks facing the area where the teacher conducts instruction. More **student-centered arrangements** include a horseshoe seating arrangement, a group pod arrangement, or a paired arrangement. A **horseshoe seating arrangement** is conducive to student-centered instruction because it allows the students to face each other and the instructor to move around the classroom easily. This setup facilitates classroom discussions and encourages interactions between instructors and students and among peers. The **group pod** or **paired-pod arrangement** is useful for student-centered instruction like small group work. This arrangement is also helpful when students need to rotate through lesson stages or work in small groups on projects. Effective teachers do not use one seating arrangement for the entire year. Best practices indicate that seating arrangements should change and be tied to the intent of lesson objectives.

Determining the Special Education Setting Placement

Special education setting placement is determined in a student's Individualized Education Program (IEP), as specified by the Individuals with Disabilities Education Act (IDEA). IDEA requires that students be placed in **general education classrooms** to the maximum extent possible. Students should be placed in environments that are most appropriate for them, known as the **least restrictive environment**. If students can be educated in general education classrooms (**inclusion**) when provided with appropriate accommodations, they can be placed in general education classrooms. When students with disabilities need modifications to curriculum that are significantly below grade level or different than their peers, the students may be placed in **resource rooms** for remedial instruction. However, the students may also participate in the general education curriculum with modified work that meets their current abilities. For example, a student who struggles in math can use a calculator accommodation in the inclusion setting. A student whose math skills are two grade levels below the skills of same-aged peers may be placed in an inclusion setting with modifications or receive instruction in a resource room.

Function of a Multidisciplinary Team-Teaching Model

The three disciplinary team models include a multidisciplinary team, an interdisciplinary team, and a transdisciplinary team. The **multidisciplinary team** is usually composed of the special educator, general education teacher, parents, paraprofessionals, principal, and school psychologist. As a whole, this team presents a comprehensive group of expertise, qualifications, and skills. In the multidisciplinary team model, these professionals do not collaborate, but instead work alongside each other to pursue a **common goal** for the individual student with special needs. The multidisciplinary team model is effective for evaluating a student for referral for special education, completing pre-referral testing, and completing an Individualized Education Program or Evaluation Team Report. Sometimes this team is referred to as the child study team or student support team. In this model, professionals usually pull out students to work with them individually. Parents and legal guardians are a part of this process. Professionals working with the student should openly communicate their processes and the results of any evaluations or informal observations.

Interdisciplinary Team Model

An interdisciplinary team model features the **general education teacher** providing all curriculum and accommodations for a student with an Individualized Education Program. In this model, the special educator and other professionals relevant to the education of the student collaborate to ensure that the curriculum meets the needs of the student and the accommodations are appropriate. This model is not a team-teaching model. Advantages of this model include the collaboration of all IEP team members towards a common goal and the student's needs being addressed by one teacher instead of several different teachers or professionals. The disadvantages of this model include difficulties with collaboration between professionals and issues with delivering related services to students who need them. Related service provision sometimes includes one-on-one instruction, which requires the student to be pulled out for a certain amount of time during general education instruction. This model may also not be appropriate for students with intense needs, as they often require **individualized education** in order to meet IEP goals. They may also require specific accommodations and modifications not suitable for the general education classroom.

Transdisciplinary Team-Teaching Model

In this model, professionals working with the student work together collaboratively to ensure the individual needs of the student are met. The **special educator** may teach in the general education classroom, delivering instruction to both students with and without disabilities. This model features a team-teaching experience for classroom students, where the special educator and general educator may take turns teaching. The presence of the special educator in the general education setting means the special educator can offer advice for **accommodating** the students with special needs in the classroom. Additionally, this model provides opportunities for teachers and other professionals to communicate consistently about students' progress, share ideas, and work collaboratively to solve any issues that arise. The effectiveness of this model relies heavily on the collaboration of the special educator and the general educator addressing the major features of this team-teaching model.

Advantages and Disadvantages of Team-Teaching Models

Students with and without disabilities present a variety of **learning abilities** in the general education classroom. One advantage of team-teaching models in this setting is being able to target the unique abilities, learning methods, and skills that each student brings to the classroom. Another advantage is effective classroom management. In an **effective team-teaching model**, one teacher provides the instruction, while the other practices classroom management skills to minimize disruptions and promote a safe learning environment. This model encourages class participation, facilitates group activities, and provides multiple means of engagement for learning content. One disadvantage is there may be an offset between the teachers sharing a class. When one teacher is not open to multiple methods of delivering instruction, the team-teaching approach is ineffective. Planning and making group decisions regarding curriculum can be time consuming and stressful in a team-teaching environment.

Lifting Guidelines for Students Who Require Physical Lifting

Teachers and paraprofessionals may encounter students with physical disabilities who require **assisted transfers**. In some circumstances, students must be **lift-assisted** from their wheelchairs in order to participate in physical therapy or floor activities. While this practice is more common in low-incidence classrooms and not always a job requirement, it is important to know school guidelines for **lifting techniques** to keep staff and students safe. Knowing school guidelines for lifting can also help prevent back injuries from occurring. Physical therapists working with the students should be consulted before attempting student lifts. They are trained professionals who know specific procedures for lifting students in order to keep the students and staff members safe. Every school district has policies for lift-assisted student transfers. Each student should be evaluated to determine if a one-person lift or two-person lift is needed. Two-person lifts are for heavier students, and some school districts do not allow two-person lifts for safety reasons.

How Cooperative Learning Works

Cooperative learning is an interpersonal group learning process where students learn concepts by working together in **small groups**. Cooperative learning involves collaboration among small groups to achieve common goals. With **formal cooperative learning**, an instructor oversees the learning of lesson material or completion of assignments for students in these small groups. With **informal cooperative learning**, the instructor supervises group activities by keeping students cognitively active but does not guide instruction or assignments. For example, a teacher might use a class period to show a movie but provide a list of questions for students to complete during the movie. In the special education classroom, cooperative learning is helpful when students need specific skills targeted or remediated. It is also helpful for separating students who are learning different content at different levels. For example, a cooperative learning activity may involve multiple groups of students with differing levels of mathematic abilities. Group work also promotes development of interpersonal skills as students interact with one another.

Benefit of Multiple Modality Instruction and Activities

The purpose of multiple modality instruction is to engage students by offering different ways to learn the same material. **Multiple modality teaching** also addresses students' unique learning styles. Learning modalities are generally separated into four categories: **visual** (seeing), **auditory** (hearing), **kinesthetic** (moving), and **tactile** (touch) modalities. This way of teaching targets students who may have deficits in one or more modalities. It is also helpful for students who struggle in one or more of the learning categories. If a student struggles with understanding content that is presented visually, a lesson that includes auditory, kinesthetic, and tactile components may engage learning. Additionally, presenting lesson material and activities in a multi-modal approach helps improve student memory and retention by solidifying concepts through multiple means of engagement. This approach is also useful for students with **attention disorders** who may struggle in environments where one mode of teaching is used. The multiple modality approach ensures that activities, such as kinesthetic or tactile activities, keep more than one sense involved with the learning process.

Components of a Successful Team-Teaching Model

A successful team-teaching model is one where the teachers involved set clear, effective, specific **goals** for performance. These goals must demonstrate clarity. All team-teaching members must be clear on the components of the goals and their potential outcomes. Clear goals allow team members and students to know what they are working towards as a classroom. Goals should be specific and measurable. **Goal criteria** should be qualified in percentages or quantities. This provides hard evidence for how effectively the team-teaching classroom is meeting the goals. Challenging goals set high expectations for what the team needs to work towards. Challenging goals ensure that team members and classroom students are working to achieve goals right outside their ability levels. Goals that are too challenging can be frustrating for all team members and students. A successful team-teaching model also reflects **commitment** from team members and any other professionals involved in the classroom.

Classroom Timing, Schedule, and Organization Accommodations

Timing, schedule, and organizational accommodations change the ways students with disabilities have access to classrooms with the fewest barriers to learning. Students who need these accommodations receive them as written statements in their Individualized Education Programs, 504 Plans, or as teachers see fit during classroom time. **Timing accommodations** allow students more time to complete tasks or tests and/or process instructions. They also allow students to access frequent breaks during assignments or tests. **Schedule accommodations** include taking tests in chunks over periods of time or several days, taking test sections in different orders, and/or taking tests during specific times of day. **Organizational skill accommodations** include assistance with time management, marking texts with highlighters, maintaining daily assignment or work schedules, and/or receiving study skills instruction. When accommodations are written in a student's IEP, the student has access to them for state standardized tests. When and how accommodations are put into place is left to the discretion of the teacher unless specifically written in the student's IEP or 504 Plan.

Creating Inclusive Learning Environments That Address Unique Needs

Effective inclusive environments abide by the **Universal Design for Learning framework**. Special educators and general educators can work together to create learning environments that are accessible to the unique needs of students with language or physical needs. This can be done by providing **multiple ways** for students to access lesson concepts, express learned concepts, and engage in the learning process. For students with language barriers, signs, symbols, pictures, and learning concepts may have different meanings than they do for students without language barriers. Keeping this in mind, teachers can address UDL guidelines for students with **language barriers** by providing diverse ways to activate prior knowledge, emphasizing key learning elements, and using visuals to guide the learning process. For students with **physical barriers**, teachers can level the learning process by making their physical classroom environments accessible and providing different ways for students to express what they have learned. In general, teachers

59

abiding by UDL framework would have these supports in place in order to ensure that the needs of diverse learners are met.

Fostering Positive and Inclusive Learning Environments Addressing Students with Learning or Cognitive Needs

Whether in the general education classroom or special education classroom, the Universal Design for Learning model should foster **positive and inclusive learning environments**. General education and special education teachers can take measures to ensure the UDL concept is implemented to address the unique needs of students with **cognitive or behavioral needs**. Since each student presents different needs, a one-size-fits-all approach to learning is not suitable or UDL compliant for these students. Special educators and general educators should openly communicate about the unique learning needs of the students with learning or cognitive needs. General strategies include receiving regular **input from special educators** on how to best meet the needs of the students in the classroom. This includes sharing information with any **paraprofessionals and aides** regarding how to assist the students in the general education classroom. UDL base strategies include the general educators providing multiple means by which students can complete the assignments. Students with cognitive disabilities may also benefit from the use of concrete examples and instruction, especially when addressing abstract concepts.

Fostering Positive and Inclusive Learning Environments Addressing Students with Behavioral Needs

The **Universal Design for Learning (UDL) concepts** can be implemented to reduce challenging behavior in the classroom. They can also be used to help students with behavioral needs find success in the general education classroom. **Lack of student engagement** is compatible with the presentation of **challenging behaviors**. When UDL concepts are demonstrated appropriately, engagement can improve. Providing **multiple means of representation** is one UDL strategy for improving engagement and challenging behavior. This means the classroom teacher provides multiple ways of presenting the teaching material in order to engage as many students as possible. Teachers that provide multiple means of representation look to activate prior knowledge and help students make sense of the current content. UDL compliant strategies also include providing **multiple means of expression**. Teachers applying UDL principles recognize that differentiating activities and assignments addresses a variety of abilities and learning styles. UDL compliant teachers should also provide **multiple means of engagement**. Successful engagement in learning can often offset challenging behaviors by helping students focus on lesson material. Offering both challenging and simplistic work options and making engaging, solid connections to past and/or future lesson content can minimize the possibility of problems arising in the classroom.

Instructional Practices in Exceptional Student Education

Teaching Strategies for Students Learning at Different Educational Levels

Learning styles of students differ, regardless of whether or not the students have disabilities. When addressing groups of students in inclusion settings, it is important for teachers to organize and implement teaching strategies that address learning at **different educational levels**. Students generally fall into one or more learning modes. Some are visual learners, some are auditory learners, some are kinesthetic or tactile learners, and some learn best using a combination of these approaches. Teachers can address students' educational levels by creating lessons that allow learning to take place visually, auditorily, and kinesthetically. **Visual learners** have preferences for seeing information that has been visually organized, such as seeing information presented in graphic organizers or diagrams. **Auditory learners** prefer information presented in spoken words. Lessons that target auditory learners provide opportunities for students to engage in conversations and/or question material. **Kinesthetic learners** prefer a hands-on approach to learning. These learners prefer to try out new tasks and learn as they go. Lessons that include opportunities for these three types of learning to occur can successfully target different educational levels.

Components of a Differentiated Curriculum

Differentiated instruction is different from individualized instruction. It targets the strengths of classroom students and can work well in both special education and general education settings. **Differentiated instruction** is also useful for targeting the needs of students with **learning and attention deficits**. With differentiated instruction, teachers adjust their instructional processes to meet the needs of the individual students. Teaching strategies and classroom management skills are based largely on each particular class of students instead of using methods that may have been successful in the past. Teachers can differentiate content, classroom activities, student projects, and the learning environments. For example, students may be encouraged to choose topics of personal interest to focus on for projects. Students are held to the same standards but have many choices in terms of project topics. **Differentiated content** means teachers provide access to a variety of resources to encourage student choice over what and how they learn. **Differentiated learning environments** are flexible to meet the ever-changing needs of the students.

Differentiated Instruction

Differentiated instruction is effective in general education settings, team-teaching settings, and special education settings because it targets the **strengths** of classroom students. Differentiated instruction is used to target the different ways that students learn instead of taking a one-size-fits-all approach. Differentiated instruction is used in lieu of individualized instruction because it uses a variety of instructional approaches and allows students access to a variety of materials to help them access the curriculum. **Effective differentiated instruction** includes small group work, reciprocal learning, and continual assessment.

Small group work allows for the individual learning styles and/or needs of students to be addressed. In small groups, students receive instruction by rotating through different sized groups. In **reciprocal learning**, students play the role of the teacher, instructing the class by sharing what they know and asking content questions of their peers. Teachers who practice **continual assessment** can determine if their differentiated instructional methods are effective or if they need to be changed. Assessments can determine what needs to be changed in order for students to participate in effective classroom environments.

61

Teaching Communication to Students Who Are Nonverbal

Nonverbal students have extra challenges in addition to learning content. These students may need extra instruction in academic areas as well as specialized instruction in the area of communication skills. Students with **nonverbal disabilities** may also need social skills instruction, struggle with abstract concepts, and dislike changes to their routines. Teachers can **facilitate learning** for nonverbal students by making changes to their classroom environments, teaching strategies for comprehending concepts, and providing materials to accommodate their needs. Teachers can also provide accommodations and/or modifications to classwork and tests to make the content accessible to nonverbal students. Additionally, teachers can assist nonverbal students by taking measures to prevent undesirable behaviors from occurring. Using visuals to represent actions, words, or concepts is a helpful instructional strategy for teaching nonverbal students, especially when teaching new material.

Co-Teaching Models

Co-teaching models are utilized in collaborative, inclusive teaching settings that include students with and without disabilities. General educators teach alongside special educators and hold all students to the same educational standards. In successful co-teaching settings, these models are used interchangeably. In the **One Teach/One Support model**, one instructor teaches a lesson while the other instructor supports students who have questions or need assistance. A **Parallel Teaching model** involves a class being split into two groups, with one instructor teaching each group. The **Alternative Teaching model** may be appropriate in situations where it is necessary to instruct small groups of students. In this model, one instructor teaches a large group of students while the other provides instruction to a smaller group of students. In **Station Teaching**, students are split into small groups and work in several teaching centers while both instructors provide support. Teachers participating in **Team-Teaching** collaboratively plan, implement lesson content, facilitate classroom discussions, and manage discipline. These models all take place in the inclusive classroom setting and are intended to meet the needs of diverse groups of learners.

Intervention Strategies for the Instruction of Students with Multiple Disabilities

Working with students with multiple disabilities can be challenging to manage. However, strategies used in other special education settings can be implemented to promote the success of students with multiple disabilities. Effective strategies include:

- setting **long-term goals**, which may last for a few years depending on how long students are in the same classrooms.
- working **collaboratively** with team members, like paraprofessionals and related services professionals, to ensure that the students' educational objectives are carried out consistently between all adults.
- developing and maintaining **group goals** that the adults and students in the classrooms can strive to achieve together.
- working with students and paraprofessionals and consulting paraprofessionals frequently for **feedback**.
- demonstrating **patience** when waiting for children to respond or complete tasks.
- learning about how students **communicate**, which may involve gestures, a Picture Exchange Communication System, or other methods.
- driving instructional and educational goals based on how students **learn best**.
- considering how students will **respond** when designing lessons, including accounting for response time during instruction.

Remedial Instruction vs. Special Education

Though the terms are sometimes used interchangeably, receiving remedial instruction does not always equal special education. The difference between remedial instruction and special education has a lot to do with the intellectual levels of the students. In **remedial instruction**, a student has average or better than average intellectual abilities but may struggle with **skills** in one or more content areas. When schools or teachers offer remedial instructional programs or opportunities in the classroom, they offer one-on-one instruction to students who are falling behind. Remedial programs are often mainstreamed into general education classrooms to address the varying learning abilities of classroom students. Remedial instruction can be delivered by general education teachers. **Special education** programs address the needs of students who may have lower intellectual abilities that require individualized instruction. Students in special education have **disabilities** that are eligible according to the Individuals with Disabilities Education Act and use Individualized Education Programs. Unlike remedial instruction, special education requires qualified and credentialed special educators to decide how to best provide interventions in classroom settings for students with disabilities.

Teaching Social Interactions to Students Who Are Nonverbal

Students who are nonverbal may have access to **communication systems** implemented by trained professionals. Teachers, caretakers, and other professionals work with the students to use the communication systems effectively. The goal of a communication system is to teach a nonverbal student how to "talk" and engage in **age-appropriate social skills**. In order for nonverbal students to learn appropriate social interactions, they must spend time learning communication skills, just as they learn academic content. Communication skills can be taught in isolation or occur within students' daily activities. Giving nonverbal students opportunities to foster communication skills in **familiar environments** ensures that they learn how to socially interact appropriately. Teachers, caregivers, and other professionals must demonstrate how to use communication systems to engage in conversations, make requests, and answer questions. Most importantly, nonverbal students must be instructed to **access** their "words" (communication systems) at all times throughout the school and home environments.

Remedial Instruction vs. Compensatory Approaches to Intervention

Compensatory interventions can be offered in the form of programs or services that help children with special needs or children who are at risk. The compensatory approach is different from remedial instruction because remedial instruction involves the breaking of concepts or tasks into smaller chunks and reteaching information. The **remedial approach** focuses on repetition and developing or reinforcing certain skills. The **compensatory approach** is implemented when a remedial approach is not working. It focuses on building upon children's strengths and working with or around their weaknesses. Tools such as audiobooks, text-to-speech software, speech recognition software, and other types of assistive technology are compensatory accommodations that provide free and appropriate educations for children with disabilities who might otherwise continue to demonstrate skill deficits without these tools. Compensatory approaches and remedial instruction can and should be delivered at the same time to ensure that children with disabilities are meeting their potential.

Levels of Bloom's Taxonomy of Learning Domains

Bloom's Taxonomy of Learning Domains is a tool that can be used for instructional planning, curriculum planning, and assessment. It is used to promote and elicit higher levels of thinking instead of relying on rote memorization. Bloom's Taxonomy can enhance instructional experiences for students by helping them to extend their **thinking skills**. This taxonomy is a useful tool for teachers wanting to improve students' thinking abilities. The taxonomy includes a list of **cognitive skills** ranking from lower-order thinking to higher-order thinking. **Remembering** is the lowest level on the taxonomy. This involves simply remembering or recalling information. **Comprehending** is the next level, which involves thinking about and understanding information. When students demonstrate **application**, the next level, they show that they can use information and apply it to real-life interactions. In the **analyzing** level, students are able to categorize, compare, and contrast information. Students demonstrate the second to last level, **evaluating**, by making decisions and demonstrating judgement. **Creating** is the last level, which involves using prior knowledge and generalizing it to new concepts.

Mapping

Concept maps are visual organizers that help students with understanding and comprehension. They are generally easy to create and implement. Concept maps should be used before approaching new learning concepts. The purpose of a concept map is to help students organize new information and make connections between other content, thoughts, and ideas. Concept maps can be constructed as part of **teacher-led instruction**, which is a strategy that may be beneficial for younger grades. They can also be constructed independently or in small groups and then discussed as a class, which is a strategy more beneficial for children in higher grades. Concept mapping starts with **identifying major concepts** from reading selections or texts. Then the major ideas are sorted into **categories**, which can be adjusted as the process continues. Arrows or other visuals can be used to demonstrate how the ideas are connected. The last integral part of the concept mapping process is the **sharing piece**, when students reflect and talk about the processes and concept maps.

Culturally Responsive Teaching and Instruction

Culturally responsive teaching (**CRT**) involves teachers implementing instruction in a variety of culturally diverse ways in order to target all students. CRT teachers respect their own cultures and the cultures of others by taking the applicable cultures into consideration during planning and instruction. CRT instruction is student centered, considers students' unique abilities and strengths, and helps build and maintain student confidence in their specific cultures. CRT instruction is about reflecting cultural pride, learning styles, and tools. Successful CRT instruction allows all students to **engage** more and **comprehend** content that applies to them. Games created to address learning objectives require attention and processing and can teach skills that emphasize use of cultural tools to solve problems. Social learning helps students become responsible for their own learning processes and develop cultural skills. Benefits of CRT include establishing inclusive classroom environments, encouraging individual development and decision-making, assisting with overall comprehension, and putting a greater emphasis on the value of learning.

Voice Recognition Software

Voice recognition software and communication software can assist students who struggle with speaking or communicating. **Voice recognition software** works through computers and allows people to speak commands into microphones instead of using keyboards. This feature creates a **least restrictive environment** for a student with a disability because it removes the sometimes challenging aspect of using a keyboard while working on a computer. Voice recognition software allows users to carry out commands such as opening documents, saving documents, and moving the mouse cursor. It also allows users to "write" sentences and paragraphs by speaking into the microphones in word processing programs. In order for voice recognition software to be effective, the user must learn to dictate words separately into a microphone. This ensures that the correct word is heard and dictated by the voice-to-text software. Some programs collect information and familiarize themselves with people's particular voice qualities. Over time, the systems learn to adapt to people's voices, and the systems become more efficient.

Effectively Instructing Students Using Assistive Technology

Assistive technology (**AT**) refers to tools effective for teaching students with learning disabilities, as they address a number of potential special needs. The purpose of AT is to level the playing field for students with **learning disabilities**, particularly when they are participating in general education classrooms. AT can address learning difficulties in math, listening, organization, memory, reading, and writing. **AT for listening** can assist students who have difficulties processing language. For example, a personal listening device can help a student hear a teacher' voice more clearly. **AT for organization and memory** can help students with self-management tasks, such as keeping assignment calendars or retrieving information using hand-held devices. **AT for reading** often include text-to-speech devices that assist with students' reading fluency, decoding, comprehension, and other skill deficits. **AT for writing** assists students who struggle with handwriting or writing development. Some AT writing devices help with actual handwriting, while others assist with spelling, punctuation, grammar, word usage, or text organization.

Types of Assistive Technology Tools

Assistive technology (**AT**) tools can be separate objects and devices or tools readily available on the Internet to assist in the learning of students with disabilities. The purpose of AT tools is to provide students with disabilities **equal access to the curriculum** by accommodating their individual needs to promote positive outcomes. **Personal listening devices (PLDs)**, sometimes called FM systems, are devices that clarify teachers' words. With a PLD, a teacher speaks into a small microphone, and the words transmit clearly into a student's headphone or earpiece. **Sound field systems** amplify teachers' voices to eliminate sound issues in the classroom environments. **Noise-cancelling headphones** are useful for students who need to work independently and limit distractions or behavioral triggers. **Audio recorders** allow students to record lectures or lessons and refer back to the recordings at their own pace. Some note-taking applications will transcribe audio into written words. Captioning is available to pair visual words with spoken words. **Text-to-speech (TTS) software** lets students see and hear words at the same time. TTS and audiobook technology can help students with fluency, decoding, and comprehension skills.

Instructing Nonverbal Students on the Use of Augmentative and Alternative Communication Systems

Students with communication disorders may often require the use of augmentative or alternative communication systems. Communication systems are used to help the students effectively demonstrate **expressive and receptive language** and engage in **social skills**. Teaching appropriate communication skills is a collaborative effort between the students' caretakers, teachers, and other professionals. Typically, **speech services** are written into students' Individualized Education Programs (IEPs), and the services are delivered by **speech language pathologists (SLPs)**. Depending on how it is written in the IEPs, the SLPs may work one-on-one with students or work with the teachers to incorporate speech and language skills throughout students' school days. In order for communication systems to work for nonverbal students, measures must be taken to ensure that the particular systems are appropriate for what the students need. It is important for the caretakers, teachers, other professionals, and even classmates to model using the devices so the students can learn how to "talk" appropriately. Students must also have constant access to the systems and receive consistent opportunities to communicate with the systems at home and at school.

Use of Visual Representation Systems with Students with Autism

Assistive technology (AT) helps increase learning opportunities for students with autism by eliminating educational barriers to learning. AT can help improve students' expressive communication skills, attention skills, motivational skills, academic skills, and more. **Visual representation systems** in the form of objects, photographs, drawings, or written words provide concrete representations of words for students with autism. Visual representations, such as simple pictures paired with words, can be used to create visual schedules for students with autism. Photographs can be used to help students learn the names of people, places, or vocabulary words. Written words should be paired with the visual representations in order to create links between the concrete objects and the actual words. The goal is for the students to eventually recognize the words without the pictures. Visual representation systems can also help facilitate easier transitions between activities or places, which can be difficult for students with autism.

Benefits of Vocational/Career Education

Students with disabilities often participate in vocational or career and technical education in order to gain **independent living skills**. Often, schools and communities offer services for vocational or career and technical education that provide vocational or career training for people with disabilities. These programs offer students **job-specific skills training** and opportunities to earn certifications, diplomas, or certificates. They often involve **hands-on learning experiences** focused on building skills specific to certain occupations. These programs are beneficial to students with disabilities, as they tend to struggle with grasping abstract concepts learned in typical classroom environments. Hands-on training in vocational or career education programs can be a meaningful way for students with disabilities to both learn academic concepts and gain living skills needed to function in post-graduate life. Vocational and technical education opportunities also offer alternatives for students with disabilities who might otherwise drop out of high school. These programs also serve as a viable option for younger students to work towards, as most vocational or career education programs are offered to students in upper grade levels.

Supporting Classroom Transitions

Transitioning to life after high school can be a difficult process, particularly for students with disabilities. It is important for teachers to facilitate and support these **transitions** before students exit their special education programs. **Structured learning environments** that include independent workstations and learning centers provide opportunities for independent learning to occur. **Independent workstations** give students chances to practice previously introduced concepts or perform previously introduced tasks. **Learning centers** provide small group settings where new skills can be taught. Students can also rotate through different learning centers that offer art lessons, focus on academic skills, or provide breaks or leisure activities. **Classroom layout** also plays an important role. Teachers should plan their classroom layouts based on individual student needs in order to create comfortable, predictable environments for students with disabilities. **Visual schedules** help students transition between centers by providing them with concrete schedule references.

Vocational Skills Needed to Be Successful in Work Environments

Informal vocational training often begins before students even get to high school. Teachers include informal vocational training skills in their classrooms by teaching academic and communication skills. **Academic skills** can both spark and strengthen students' career interests and provide learning platforms to build upon. **Communication skills** generalize to work environments when students learn appropriate communication skills, like how to give and follow instructions and process information. **Social and interpersonal skills**, like problem-solving abilities and learning how to participate in phone conversations, are important for teaching students how to perform in workplaces. Students also need to learn important **vocational and occupational skills** required by most jobs, such as how to interact appropriately with coworkers and keep track of worked hours. Students also need formal or informal training in completing resumes, cover letters, and tax forms. Training may also include interviewing practice and job search guidance.

Resources to Promote Successful Transitions to Life after High School

In some states, **statements of transition** should be included on Individualized Education Programs (IEPs) at age 14 for students with disabilities. In most states, the Individuals with Disabilities Education Act mandates that transition plans be put in place for students on IEPs at age 16 and every year thereafter. Some schools and communities have programs and/or resources available to facilitate students' successful transitions to life after high school. Throughout the transition process, it is important that students and their caregivers participate in any decision-making processes. **Vocational education courses**, sometimes called career and technical education (CTE) courses, offer academic course alternatives. The courses usually specialize in specific trades or occupations. They can serve to spark or maintain students' interests in vocational fields. Some schools offer **post-secondary enrollment options (PSEO)**, where students can participate in college courses, earning both high school and college credits. **Career assessments**, including interest inventories and formal and informal vocational assessments, serve to gauge students' career interests. These can be worked into students' transitional goals on their IEPs and should be conducted frequently as students' interests change.

Components of a Transition Plan

Per federal law, transition plans are required to be part of a student's Individualized Education Program during the year the student turns 16 years old. The **transition plan components** include postsecondary goals and transition services. The purpose of the goals is to state what a student wants to achieve after high school. The four goal areas are vocational training, post-secondary education, employment, and independent living. **Transition goals** must be results oriented and measurable. Goals can be general, but the transition activities need to be quantified to reflect what the student can complete in the IEP year. It is common for interests to change from year to year. Therefore, goals and plans may change as well. **Transition services** are determined once the goals are established. Transition services include types of instruction the student will receive in school, related services, community experiences, career or college counseling, and help with adaptive behavior skills. Goals and transition services must be reviewed and updated each year. Academic goals in the IEP can also support transition goals. For example, academic math goals can focus on money management skills as part of a transition plan.

Purpose and Implications of a Transition Plan on the IEP

In most states, a transition plan should be included on the Individualized Education Program (IEP) for a student with a disability the year the student turns 16 years old. As mandated by the Individuals with Disabilities Education Act, a transition plan should include **goals and services** specific to the student's individual needs. The purpose of a transition plan on a student's IEP is to help guide and prepare the student for post-secondary employment, education, and independent living. A transition plan is driven by the student's **interests**, which can be gathered via formal and informal career assessments, such as interest inventories. A transition plan includes **goals** specific to a student's expressed interests, which can or will be achieved within the IEP year. Successful goals are objective, measurable, and specifically related to a student's expressed interests. These goals can include goals for post-secondary employment, education, and/or independent living, depending on the needs and interests of the specific student. Transition goals can also include student goals for vocational training.

Factors That Influence Successful Transitions to Post-Secondary Life

Students, parents or legal guardians, teachers, school professionals, and sometimes community members are key **factors** in successful transitions to post-secondary life for students with disabilities. Factors that influence students' successful transitions include participation in standards-based education, work preparation and career-based learning experiences, and experience with leadership skills. Other factors that influence successful transitions include access to and experience with **community services**, such as mental health and transportation services. Lastly, **family involvement and support** are key factors in facilitating successful transitions for students with disabilities. Standards-based education ensures that students receive consistent and clear expectations with curriculum that is aligned to the Universal Design for Learning standards. Exposure to work preparation and career-based learning experiences ensures that students receive opportunities to discover potential career interests and/or hobbies. Connections and experiences with community activities provide students with essential post-secondary independent living skills. Family involvement and support ensure that students have advocates for their needs and interests. Families can also help students connect with school and community-based supports that facilitate their career interests.

Including Measurable and Challenging Objectives in Lesson Plans

Lesson objectives should be **SMART**, meaning they should be specific, measurable, attainable, relevant, and time based. When teachers plan lessons, SMART objectives provide the framework to effectively execute the lesson plans. Specific objectives describe exactly what will be taught within the time frame of the lesson. Specific objectives answer **"W" questions**, such as the questions listed below.

- **What** do I want to accomplish?
- **Why** is this goal important?
- **Who** is involved?
- **Where** is it located?
- **Which** resources are available?

Measurable objectives are important for staying on task and tracking progress. **Attainable** objectives are created with students' strengths and needs in mind. Attainable objectives should keep in mind what students can realistically accomplish within the lesson time frame. Achievable objectives spell out how the goals will be accomplished. A good attainable objective is challenging but realistically achievable based on students' abilities. **Relevant** objectives should build upon prior knowledge and matter to the teacher and the students. Relevant objectives promote student interest and engagement. **Time-bound** objectives set deadlines and help prioritize objectives.

Positive Behavioral Support Process

Behavior Issues of Students and Intervention Strategies

Behavior issues occur with students with and without disabilities. However, they may occur more frequently or to a higher degree for some students with disabilities. Behavior issues are often a **manifestation** of a child's disability. For example, students with Attention Deficit Hyperactivity Disorder may present with attention and focus issues and impulsivity. **Common behavior issues** include:

- emotional outbursts
- inattention and inability to focus
- impulsivity
- aggression
- abusive language
- oppositional defiance
- lying or stealing
- threatening adults or peers

Other behavior issues may include inappropriate sexual behavior, inability to control sexual behavior, self-harm, or self-harm attempts. Behavior issues can be **avoided** or **remediated** with classroom management skills, like setting clear and consistent classroom goals, setting time limits, and providing visuals to assist with transitions or concepts. When a student is in an aggressive state, it is important for the teacher to remain calm, provide choices for the student, and restate the consequences of any aggressive outbursts.

Managing Students with Emotional Disturbances

Managing a classroom of students with emotional disorders can be challenging and unpredictable. Students with emotional disorders have Individualized Education Program goals that focus on **controlling** or **monitoring** their daily behavior choices. However, this does not always mean they will engage in meeting these goals. It is important for educators to know how to **manage** issues students with emotional disorders may bring to the classroom. When creating resources and lesson plans, an educator should:

- establish a **safety plan**, which includes knowing how to implement a **crisis prevention plan**.
- maintain an environment that reduces **stimulation** and provides **visual cues** for expected behavior.
- implement **intervention-based strategies** for managing student behavior.
- collect and use **data** to identify triggers, track behaviors, and recognize successful strategies that produced positive outcomes.
- practice open **communication** about classroom expectations to students, parents, and other teachers.

Special education teachers can be good resources for many of these components, especially when students with emotional disorders are in inclusive settings.

Concept of Antecedents, Behavior, and Consequences as Stimuli Used in Behavior Analysis

Antecedents and consequences play a role in behavioral analysis, which is important for evaluating the behaviors of students. The purpose of behavior analysis is to gather information about a specific behavior demonstrated by a student. **Antecedents** refer to the actions or events that occur before the behavior occurs. It is important to recognize antecedents for behaviors to better understand under what circumstances the behavior is occurring. The **behavior** is the undesirable action that occurs as a result of the antecedent. **Consequences** are what happens immediately after the behavior occurs. These can be natural or enforced. A certain consequence might be what the student desires by doing the behavior. Understanding the antecedents, behavior, and consequences and the relationships between them for a particular behavior allows a professional to determine how to minimize or eliminate the behavior. In some circumstances, antecedents can be manipulated, changed, or removed in order to avoid the undesired behavior. Consequences can be manipulated, changed, or removed in order to avoid reinforcing the undesired behavior.

Behavior Rating Scale Assessments

Behavior rating scales address the needs of students with emotional disorders who are referred to special education. Problems with behavior are often the reason a student has been referred for special education. Behavior rating scales are used in determining a student's **eligibility** for special education. Behavior rating scales are also useful in addressing **undesirable behaviors** demonstrated by students with other disorders in special education. They are similar to adaptive behavior scales because teachers or other professionals can administer the scales with little training as long as they are familiar with the students. Behavior rating scales help rate the frequency and intensity of the behaviors for a particular student. Behavior frequency and intensity are often rated with numbered rating scales. They serve as starting points for learning more about a student's behavior so that behavior interventions and management can take place. These scales are **norm-referenced**, so the outcomes of the behavior rating scales are compared to the behaviors of others.

Negative and Positive Reinforcement Related to Applied Behavior Analysis

Part of applied behavior analysis is applying negative and positive reinforcement strategies. **Reinforcement** is a process that involves increasing the possibility of a desired behavior occurring. The goal of reinforcement is for the desired behavior to continue occurring in the future. **Positive reinforcement** works by providing a desired **reward** for a desired behavior. By reinforcing the desired behavior when it is exhibited, it increases the likelihood that the behavior will occur in the future. For example, parents may give a child an allowance for doing chores, and the allowance is the positive reinforcement for the behavior (the chores). In contrast, **negative reinforcement** is when a stimulus, usually an **aversive stimulus**, is removed to enforce a desired behavior. Negative reinforcement should not be seen as a punishment because a punishment is given to decrease a behavior. With negative reinforcement, the goal is for behaviors to increase by stopping, removing, or avoiding negative outcomes. An example of negative reinforcement is making a child finish dinner before receiving a popsicle. The popsicle is the reward for demonstrating the expected behavior.

Developing Positive Behavioral Interventions and Supports

Positive behavioral intervention and support (**PBIS**) plans can be implemented in classrooms or schoolwide to encourage specific, positive outcomes in groups of students with and without disabilities. A PBIS plan, such as an anti-bullying campaign, is put in place to encourage **good**

70

behavior and/or **school safety**. The goal of a PBIS plan is to teach students appropriate behavior, just as they would learn any other academic subject. PBIS plans are put in place to teach students positive behavior or safety procedures that are incompatible with undesirable behaviors. Appropriate PBIS plans should be based on the results of data collected on targeted, large-scale behaviors. They should also be research based and proven effective. As with any behavioral plans, PBIS plans are most successful when student progress is monitored. An effective PBIS plan removes **environmental triggers** for behavior, reducing the chances of the behavior occurring in the first place. PBIS plans should change if they do not work or stop working.

Developing Functional Behavior Assessment

A functional behavior assessment (**FBA**) is a formal process used to examine student behavior. The goal of an FBA is to identify what is causing a specific behavior and evaluate how the behavior is affecting the student's educational performance. Once these factors are determined, the FBA is useful in implementing **interventions** for the specific behavior. When an FBA is developed, a student's behavior must be specifically defined. Then the teacher or other professional devises a plan for collecting data on the behavior. This is helpful in determining what may be causing the behavior, such as environmental triggers. Collected data is analyzed to determine the big picture for what may be causing the behavior. The analyzed data is used to formulate a hypothesis about what is causing the behavior, so the teacher or other professional can then implement the most appropriate plan for addressing the student's specific behavior. Often, this means implementing a **behavior intervention plan**, which includes introducing the student to actions or processes that are incompatible with the problem behavior. It is important to monitor the plan to ensure effectiveness or remediate certain steps.

Implementing Crisis Prevention Plans

Students with disabilities sometimes display symptoms of their particular disorders that require trained adults to implement **crisis prevention plans**. Some organizations, such as the Crisis Prevention Institute, specialize in crisis prevention and intervention training for professionals. Crisis prevention plans are put in place to help the students **avoid** the behaviors before they occur. The goal is to keep the students functioning appropriately in their environments by removing or being aware of possible **behavioral triggers**. Crisis prevention plans are important to have in place for when students' behaviors become safety concerns. It is helpful to recognize warning signs that crises may be starting, and this can be done by providing interventions when people exhibit behaviors that are typical for them. Clear structure and expectations allow students to understand direct consequences for undesired choices, prior to crisis mode. When students enter crisis mode, the crisis prevention plans provide clear processes that professionals can use to de-escalate the situations.

Developing Behavior Intervention Plans

A behavior intervention plan is based on a **functional behavior assessment (FBA)**. A **behavior intervention plan (BIP)** is a formal plan that follows the results of an FBA. The purpose of the BIP is to teach the student actions, behaviors, or processes that are incompatible with the problem behavior. The BIP may be included on an Individualized Education Program or 504 Plan, or components of the BIP may be written out as IEP goals. Once an FBA is conducted, a BIP is put in place that describes the behavior, lists factors that trigger the target behavior, and lists any interventions that help the student avoid the behavior. The target behavior is the behavior that needs to be changed. The interventions determined by the FBA and listed in the BIP focus on the problem behavior. The interventions include problem-solving skills for the student to use instead of demonstrating the target behavior. When the interventions fail to target the problem behavior and/or are no longer effective for targeting the behavior, an FBA must be revisited and a new BIP should be developed.

Positive Classroom Discipline Strategies

Promoting positive classroom discipline is part of effective classroom management. This involves holding students accountable for their actions, and it starts with establishing clear and consistent **consequences** when poor choices are demonstrated. Students learn to predict consequences and self-correct their behaviors. It is helpful to give **reminders** before immediately resorting to consequences. Reminders help students remember the consequences for breaking rules regarding behavior. **Pre-reminders** are one way to enforce and remind students of expectations before diving into lessons. **Nonverbal reminders**, such as looks, touches, silence, or removal, are possible ways to distract students from engaging in poor choices. Removal involves tasks like sending students to throw things away. **Spoken reminders** can be used to further encourage self-management skills and should be used as precursors for reminding students about expectations instead of delivering immediate consequences.

Promoting Appropriate Behavior in Inclusive Learning Environments

Effective classrooms have good management strategies in place that promote good learning environments and minimize disruptions. When it comes to students with disabilities, planning classroom management strategies presents different challenges. In **inclusive learning environments**, it is important for teachers to keep all students on track with their learning. General educators and special educators can demonstrate effective classroom management strategies by figuring out what is causing students to act out or misbehave. Effective teachers understand how students' special needs come into play with expected classroom behaviors. They also promote positive classroom experiences, establish clear expectations for behavior, and reinforce positive behaviors. Teachers with effective classroom management strategies demonstrate good leadership and organizational skills. They collaborate with other professionals and students' parents to ensure the success of students with special needs in their classrooms. Lastly, effective classroom management includes setting goals for inclusive classrooms to achieve. Clear goals help establish good rapport with students with special needs because they know what is expected of them.

Supporting Mental Health Issues

Students with disabilities present mental health issues in some circumstances and in some educational settings. These students may not necessarily be diagnosed with emotional disturbances, as mental health issues can occur concurrently with other disabilities. General and special educators across all special education settings can **support** these students by learning how to **recognize mental health issues** in schools. Students' mental health symptoms may fluctuate on an hourly, daily, or weekly basis. Teachers can use observations and other research-based strategies for identifying any issues. They may also already be aware of such issues or work in settings where mental health issues are predominant. Intervention techniques and supports rely on the individual needs of each specific student. Training in managing students with certain mental health disorders may also be useful. Occasionally, training in crisis prevention plans is required of teachers working with students who may become aggressive due to their disorders.

Working with Students with Physical Disabilities

Students with physical disabilities may be included in **general education classrooms** with accommodations if their disabilities do not coexist with other disabilities, such as learning

72

disabilities. They may also be placed in inclusive settings or partially inclusive settings with Individualized Education Program goals, depending on their least restrictive environments. In these settings, it is essential for educators to practice **instructional strategies** that facilitate the learning processes and accommodate the needs of students with physical disabilities. Classrooms should be arranged so they can be **navigated** easily by everyone. This includes giving students using wheelchairs adequate aisle space and work space. **Partner work** is helpful for students with physical disabilities, who may struggle with handwriting or using keyboards. Partners can assist the students with skills like note taking, which may be difficult for students with physical disabilities. Additionally, assignments can include **accommodations** or **modifications** to meet the specific needs of students with physical disabilities. For example, text-to-speech software can be provided for students who struggle with using regular keyboards.

Multiple Literacies and Communication Skills

Helping Students Develop Oral Language Abilities

Children pick up oral language skills in their home environments and build upon these skills as they grow. Early language development is a combination of genetic disposition, environment, and individual thinking processes. Children with **oral language acquisition difficulties** often experience difficulties in their **literacy skills**. Engaging students in activities that promote good oral language skills is beneficial to these skills as well as their literacy skills. **Strategies** that help students develop oral language abilities include developing appropriate speaking and listening skills, providing instruction that emphasizes vocabulary development, providing students with opportunities to communicate wants, needs, ideas, and information, creating language learning environments, and promoting auditory memory. Developing appropriate speaking and listening skills includes teaching turn-taking, awareness of social norms, and basic rules for speaking and listening. Emphasizing **vocabulary development** is a strategy that familiarizes early learners with word meanings. Providing students with opportunities to **communicate** is beneficial for developing early social skills. Teachers can create **language learning environments** by promoting literacy in their classrooms with word walls, reading circles, or other strategies that introduce language skills to students. Promoting **auditory memory** means teaching students to listen to, process, and recall information.

Components of Oral Language Development

Oral language learning begins well before students enter educational environments. It is learned first without formal instruction, with **environmental factors** being a heavy influence. Children tend to develop their own linguistic rules as a result of genetic disposition, their environments, and how their individual thinking processes develop. Components of oral language development include phonological components, semantic components, and syntactic components. **Phonological components** focus on the rules for combining sounds. **Semantic components** focus on the smallest units of sounds, morphemes, and how they combine to make up words. **Syntactic components** focus on how morphemes combine to form sentences. This complex system of phonological, semantic, and syntactic components grows and develops as children grow. **Oral language development** can be nurtured by caregivers and teachers well before children enter educational environments. Caregivers and teachers can promote oral language development by providing environments full of language development opportunities. Additionally, teaching children how conversation works, encouraging interaction among children, and demonstrating good listening and speaking skills are good strategies for nurturing oral language development.

Helping Students Monitor Errors in Oral Language

Oral language is the way people express knowledge, ideas, and feelings. As oral language develops, so do **speaking and listening skills**, which have strong connections to reading comprehension and writing skills. Oral language first develops in infancy and becomes fine-tuned with instruction as students enter grade school. Teachers can monitor **oral language errors** with progress monitoring strategies. Teachers can also help students monitor their own **oral language development** as they progress through the reading curriculum. Students can monitor their oral language by listening to spoken words in their school and home environments, learning and practicing self-correction skills, and participating in reading comprehension and writing activities. Students can also monitor oral language errors by learning oral language rules for phonics, semantics, syntax, and pragmatics.

74

These are rules for learning sounds, words, and meanings in the English language. Learning these oral language rules typically generalizes to developing appropriate oral language skills.

Expressive Language

Expressive language involves the ability to use vocabulary, sentences, gestures, and writing. **Expressive language skills** mean that people can label objects in their environments, put words in sentences, use appropriate grammar, demonstrate comprehension verbally by retelling stories, and more. This type of language is important because it allows people to express feelings, wants and needs, thoughts and ideas, and individual points of view. Expressive language helps people develop spoken and written language and promotes positive interactions with others. Expressive language goes hand in hand with **receptive language**, which is the understanding of language. Children can learn solid expressive language skills by:

- completing tasks that require attention and focus.
- developing pre-language skills, such as understanding gestures like nodding.
- developing good pragmatics.
- developing intrinsic social motivation skills.
- developing fine motor skills, which are required for students who use sign language or gestures to communicate.

Receptive Language

Receptive language refers to a person's ability to understand language. Good receptive language means a person is gathering information from the environment and processing it into meaning. People with good **receptive language skills** perceive visual information, sounds and words, basic cognitive concepts like colors and shapes, and written information (i.e. street signs) well. Receptive language is important for developing appropriate communication skills. **Strategies** to build receptive language skills in children include activities that maintain focus and attention. This requires children to participate in activities that require sustained attention free of distractions in order to improve receptive communication skills. **Pre-language skills** are skills that people use before they learn to communicate with words. Building appropriate pre-language skills is another strategy for building receptive language. Lastly, focusing on **social skills and play skills instruction** encourages opportunities for children to interact with their peers or adults. This fosters receptive language skills or targets deficits in these skills.

Stages of Language Development in Infants and Children

The first stage of language development and acquisition, the **pre-linguistic stage**, occurs during an infant's first year of life. It is characterized by the development of gestures, making eye contact, and sounds like cooing and crying. The **holophrase**, or one-word sentence stage, develops in infants between 10 and 13 months of age. In this stage, young children use one-word sentences to communicate meaning in language. The **two-word sentence stage** typically develops by the time a child is 18 months old. Each two-word sentence usually contains a verb and a modifier, such as "big balloon" or "green grass." Children in this stage use their two-word sentences to communicate wants and needs. **Multiple-word sentences** form by the time a child is two to two and a half years old. In this stage, children begin forming sentences with subjects and predicates, such as "tree is tall" or "rope is long." Grammatical errors are present, but children in this stage begin demonstrating how to use words in appropriate context. Children ages two and a half to three years old typically begin using more **complex grammatical structures**. They begin to include grammatical structures such as conjunctions and prepositions. For example, they may say, "Throw it, the ball," or "Bring me outside." By the age of five or six, children reach a stage of **adult-like language development**. They begin to use words in appropriate context and can move words around in sentences while maintaining appropriate sentence structure.

Stages of Literacy Development

The development of literacy in young children is separated into five stages. Names of these stages sometimes vary, but the stage milestones are similar. Stage 1 is the **Emergent Reader stage**. In this stage, young children ages 6 months to 6 years demonstrate skills like pretend reading, recognizing letters of the alphabet, retelling stories, and printing their names. Stage 2 is the **Novice/Early Reader stage** (ages 6–7 years). Children begin to understand the relationships between letters and sounds and written and spoken words, and they read texts containing high-frequency words. Children in this stage should develop orthographic conventions and semantic knowledge. In Stage 3, the **Decoding Reader stage**, children ages 7–9 develop decoding skills in order to read simple stories. They also demonstrate increased fluency. Stage 4 (ages 8–15 years) is called the **Fluent, Comprehending/Transitional Reader stage**. In this stage, fourth to eighth graders read to learn new ideas and information. In Stage 5, the **Expert/Fluent Reader stage**, children ages 16 years and older read more complex information. They also read expository and narrative texts with multiple viewpoints.

Implications of Literacy Development for Children with Disabilities

Literacy development is broken into five stages. Names of these stages sometimes vary.

- Stage 1 (ages 6 months to 6 years) Emergent Reader Stage
- Stage 2 (ages 6–7 years) Novice/Early Reader Stage
- Stage 3 (ages 7–9 years) Decoding Reader Stage
- Stage 4 (ages 8–15 years) Fluent, Comprehending/Transitional Reader Stage
- Stage 5 (16+ years) Expert/Fluent Reader Stage

Children may not always meet the **literacy stage milestones** during the specified ages. However, this does not always indicate a disability. Children who fall significantly behind in their literacy development, continually struggle with skill acquisition, or do not consistently retain skill instruction may be at higher risk of being identified as having **disabilities**. Furthermore, children with **speech and language disorders** are more likely to experience problems learning to read and write. These issues are typically apparent before children enter grade school but can also become evident during their early grade school years. **Early warning signs** include disinterest in shared book reading, inability to recognize or remember names of letters, difficulty understanding directions, and persistent baby talk.

Promoting Literacy During the Early Stages of Literacy Development

Teachers and parents can implement strategies at different stages of literacy development in order to build **good reading skills** in children with and without disabilities. During the **Emergent Reader stage**, teachers and parents can introduce children to the conventions of reading with picture books. They can model turning the pages, reading from left to right, and other reading conventions. Book reading at this stage helps children begin to identify letters, letter sounds, and simple words. Repetitive reading of familiar texts also helps children begin to make predictions about what they are reading. During the **Novice/Early Reader** and **Decoding Reader stages**, parents and teachers can help children form the building blocks of decoding and fluency skills by reading for meaning and emphasizing letter-sound relationships, visual cues, and language patterns. In these stages, increasing familiarity with sight words is essential. In Stage 4, the **Fluent,**

Comprehending Reader/Transitional stage, children should be encouraged to read book series, as the shared characters, settings, and plots help develop their comprehension skills. At this stage, a good reading rate (fluency) is an indicator of comprehension skills. **Expert/Fluent readers** can independently read multiple texts and comprehend their meanings. Teachers and parents can begin exposing children to a variety of fiction and non-fiction texts before this stage in order to promote good fluency skills.

Relationship Between Language Development and Early Literacy Skills

Language development and early literacy skills are interconnected. **Language concepts** begin and develop shortly after birth with infant/parent interactions, cooing, and then babbling. These are the earliest attempts at language acquisition for infants. Young children begin interacting with written and spoken words before they enter their grade school years. Before they enter formal classrooms, children begin to make **connections** between speaking and listening and reading and writing. Children with strong speaking and listening skills demonstrate strong literacy skills in early grade school. The development of **phonological awareness** is connected to early literacy skills. Children with good phonological awareness recognize that words are made up of different speech sounds. For example, children with appropriate phonological awareness can break words (i.e. "bat") into separate speech sounds (i.e. "b-a-t"). Examples of phonological awareness include rhyming (when the ending parts of words have the same or similar sounds) and alliteration (when words all have the same beginning sound). Success with phonological awareness (oral language) activities depends on adequate development of speech and language skills.

Importance of Enforcing Word Recognition

Many students with specific learning disabilities demonstrate **deficits in reading abilities**. This includes **word recognition abilities**. Teaching **word identification** is important for these students because developing age-appropriate word recognition skills is one of the essential building blocks for creating efficient readers. Children who do not develop adequate reading skills in elementary school are generally below average readers as they age in school. Most districts and teachers use **basal reading programs** that teach word recognition and phonics. Teachers often supplement basal reading programs with **instructional programs** that can be used at home and at school. These are especially useful for students with disabilities or students who are at risk and struggle with word recognition abilities. Elements of basal and supplementary reading programs include instruction for helping students make connections between letters and sounds, opportunities to become comfortable with reading, alphabetic knowledge, phonemic awareness, letter-sound correlations, word identification strategies, spelling, writing, and reading fluency.

Characteristics of Expressive Language Disabilities

Expressive language refers to a person's ability to express wants and needs. Children with **expressive language disabilities** may have trouble conversing with peers and adults and have trouble with self-expression. Answers to questions may be vague or repetitive. They may not demonstrate age-appropriate social skills with peers and adults. Children with expressive language disabilities have a limited vocabulary range and rely on familiar vocabulary words in their expressive language. They can be very quiet and seclude themselves from classroom activities due to difficulties expressing their thoughts and feelings. They may not be able to accurately express what they understand because children with expressive language difficulties have trouble speaking in sentences. Expressive language disabilities indicate issues with **language processing centers** in the brain. Children with this disability can sometimes understand language but have trouble

77

Mometrix

expressing it. Children with traumatic brain injury, dyslexia, autism, or learning disabilities demonstrate issues with expressive language.

Targeting and Implementing Social Skills Instruction

Developing good social skills is essential for lifelong student success, and people with disabilities often struggle with these skills. Addressing social skill behavior is most effective when:

- **social skill needs** are specifically identified.
- **social skills instruction** is implemented as a collaborative effort between parents and teachers.

Evaluating **developmental milestones** is helpful in targeting social skills that need to be addressed and taught. If a child with a disability is not demonstrating a milestone, such as back and forth communication, this skill can be evaluated to determine if it should be taught. However, meeting milestones is not a surefire way to measure a student's social skill ability, as some children naturally progress more slowly. Social skill deficits may be acquisition deficits, performance deficits, or fluency deficits. **Acquisition deficits** occur when a student demonstrates an absence of a skill or behavior. **Performance deficits** occur when a student does not implement a social skill consistently. A **fluency deficit** means a student needs assistance with demonstrating a social skill effectively or fluently. Once the student's social skill need is identified, teachers, parents, and other professionals can collaborate to incorporate an established routine or behavior contract or to implement applied behavior analysis.

Purposes and Benefits of Social Skills Groups

Social skills groups are useful for helping students with **social skill deficits** learn and practice appropriate skills with their peers. Social skills groups are primarily composed of similar-aged peers with and without disabilities. An adult typically leads the group and teaches students skills needed for making friends, succeeding in school and life, and sometimes obtaining and maintaining a job. Other professionals, such as school psychologists or speech language pathologists, may also lead social skills groups. Social skills groups work by facilitating **conversation** and focusing on **skill deficits**, such as reading facial cues. Social skills groups have many benefits. They can help students learn to appropriately greet others, begin conversations, respond appropriately, maintain conversations, engage in turn-taking, and request help when needed.

Receiving Special Education Services in the Least Restrictive Environment

The Individuals with Disabilities Education Act (IDEA) requires a free and appropriate public education (FAPE) to be provided in a student with a disability's **least restrictive environment (LRE)**. This means that a student who qualifies for special education should be educated in a free, appropriate, and public setting and be placed in an instructional setting that meets the LRE principle. IDEA states that LRE means students with disabilities should participate in the general education classroom "to the maximum extent that is appropriate." **Mainstreaming** and **inclusion** are two words that are associated with LRE because these are the two settings where students with disabilities can participate in the general education classroom while receiving appropriate accommodations, modifications, interventions, and/or related services. The amount of time a student spends in an LRE suitable for his or her individual needs is stated in the Individualized Education Program (IEP). The accommodations, modifications, interventions, and/or related services the student should receive are also outlined in the IEP. Students who need special education services for more than 50% of the day may be placed in instructional settings that meet their LRE needs, such as resource rooms or self-contained classrooms.

Continuum of Special Education Services

IDEA mandates that school systems must educate students with disabilities with students who do not have disabilities to the maximum extent that is appropriate. IDEA also mandates that schools may not take students out of regular education classes unless the classes are not benefitting the students. Supplementary aids and support services must be in place before students can be considered for removal. Schools must offer a **continuum of special education services** that offer a restrictive to least restrictive range. In a typical continuum of services, regular education classrooms offer the **least restrictive access** to students with disabilities. After regular education classrooms, students can be educated in resource rooms, then special classes that target specific deficits. Special schools, homebound services, and hospitals and institutions are the last three least restrictive educational options for children with disabilities. The number of students in these continuum settings decreases as restriction increases. Fewer students benefit from being educated in hospitals or institutions than in resource rooms.

Evidence-Based Methods for Promoting Self-Determination

Students with disabilities often need to be taught skills for promoting **self-determination** and **self-advocacy**. These skills may not come easily to students with specific disorders like autism. Self-determination involves a comprehensive understanding of one's own **strengths and limitations**. Self-determined people are **goal-oriented** and intrinsically motivated to **improve themselves**. Teachers can facilitate the teaching of these skills in a number of ways, starting in early elementary school. In early elementary school, teachers can promote self-determination by teaching choice-making skills and providing clear consequences for these choices. Teacher can also promote problem solving and self-management skills, like having students evaluate their own work. At the middle school and junior high level, students can be taught to evaluate and analyze their choices. They can also learn academic and personal goal-setting skills and decision-making skills. At the high school level, teachers can promote decision-making skills, involvement in educational planning (i.e. attending their Individualized Education Program meetings), and strategies like self-instruction, self-monitoring, and self-evaluation. Throughout the educational process, teachers should establish and maintain high standards for learning, focus on students' strengths, and create positive learning environments that promote choice and problem-solving skills.

Teaching Self-Awareness Skills

Students engage in private self-awareness and public self-awareness. Some students with disabilities have the additional challenge of needing instruction in **self-awareness skills**. Special educators and other professionals can facilitate the instruction of self-awareness skills by teaching students to be **aware** of their thoughts, feelings, and actions. Self-awareness also means teaching students how their thoughts, feelings, and actions **affect other people**. Students can be taught self-awareness by identifying their own strengths and weaknesses and learning to self-monitor errors in assignments. They can also be taught to identify what materials or steps are needed to complete tasks. Additionally, students can learn to recognize that other people have needs and feelings and recognize how their behaviors affect others. Students can also learn self-awareness by recognizing the limitations of their disabilities and learning to advocate for accommodations or strategies that work for them. Special educators or other professionals should frequently talk with students about their performances and encourage students to discuss their mistakes without criticism.

79

Importance of Learning Self-Advocacy Skills

Self-advocacy is an important skill to learn for people entering adulthood. For students with disabilities, **self-advocacy skills** are especially important for success in **post-secondary environments**. Teaching and learning self-advocacy skills should begin when students enter grade school and be reinforced in the upper grade levels. Students with disabilities who have the potential to enter post-secondary education or employment fields need to learn self-advocacy skills in order to **communicate** how their disabilities may affect their educational or job performances. They must also communicate the need for supports and possible accommodations in the educational, training, or employment fields. Students with disabilities who graduate or age out of their Individualized Education Programs do not receive the **educational supports** they received at the grade school level. It is essential for students to advocate for themselves in the absence of teachers or caregivers advocating for them, especially when students independently enter post-secondary employment, training, or educational environments. Many colleges, universities, communities, and work environments offer services to students with disabilities who need them, but it is up to the students to advocate for themselves and seek them out.

Providing Instruction in the Area of Functional Living Skills

Also known as life skills, functional skills are skills students need to know to live independently. Ideally, students leave high school having gained functional skills. For students with special needs, **functional skills instruction** is needed to gain independent living skills. Students with developmental disabilities or cognitive disabilities sometimes need to acquire basic living skills, such as self-feeding or toileting. **Applied behavior analysis** is a process where these skills can be broken down, modeled, and taught. These students must also learn functional math and language arts skills, such as managing money and reading bus schedules. Students may also participate in **community-based instruction** to learn skills while completing independent living tasks in the community. These skills include grocery shopping, reading restaurant menus, and riding public transportation. **Social skills instruction** is also important for these students, as learning appropriate social interactions is necessary to function with community members.

Promoting Critical Thinking Skills

Critical thinking is a self-directed thinking process that helps people make logical, reasonable judgements. This is an especially challenging skill for students with **developmental disabilities**, who often demonstrate deficits in logical thinking and reasoning abilities. In order to teach these students **critical thinking skills**, the focus should be on encouraging critical thinking across **home and school environments** and providing opportunities for students to practice this type of thinking. Teachers and parents can encourage critical thinking by implementing teaching strategies focused on fostering **creativity** in students. Instead of providing outlines or templates for lesson concepts, students can use their prior knowledge to figure out the boundaries of the lessons independently and explore new concepts. Parents and teachers should not always be quick to jump in and help students who are struggling. Sometimes the best way to help is by facilitating ways for students to solve problems without doing things for them. Opportunities for brainstorming, classifying and categorizing information, comparing and contrasting information, and making connections between topics are teaching strategies that also facilitate critical thinking skills.

Metacognitive Approach to Teaching

Metacognition refers to people's awareness and understanding of their own thinking processes. The **metacognitive approach** to teaching helps students think about their thinking processes and make sense of the world around them. Increasing their levels of **self-awareness** allows students to gain an understanding of how they feel, think, and act. This helps them optimize their educational performances because by learning more about how they feel, think, and act, they begin to understand more about how they learn. Teachers can engage students in metacognitive thinking by teaching them how to think **reflectively**. Teachers should also encourage students to recognize what they do not understand. This allows them to be comfortable with a lack of understanding and learn how to work through it. Instructors can also provide time for students to keep learning journals that note their learning progress throughout the year. Reflecting on projects and assignments, monitoring their own skills, and providing tests that target **higher level thinking objectives**, like essay tests, also promote metacognitive thinking in students.

Teaching Participation in Career-Based Education

During their schooling years, students with disabilities have the additional challenge of determining possible **career options** for life after high school. Fortunately, instruction can be provided during the school day or within after-school programs that address career-based skills. Effective **career-based programs** for students with disabilities should work collaboratively with community and school resources. Students should receive information on career options, be exposed to a range of experiences, and learn how to self-advocate. Information regarding career options can be gathered via **career assessments** that explore students' possible career interests. Students should receive exposure to **post-secondary education** to determine if it is an option that aligns with their career interests. They should also learn about basic job requirements, such as what it means to earn a living wage and entry requirements for different types of jobs. Students should be given opportunities for job training, job shadowing, and community service. It is helpful to provide students with opportunities to learn and practice **work and occupational skills** that pertain to specific job interests. Students need to learn **self-advocacy skills**, such as communicating the implications of their disabilities to employers, in order to maintain success in post-secondary work environments.

Prior Knowledge

By the time children enter school, their life experiences have shaped their understandings about how the world around them works. Activating **prior knowledge** is a way to build upon and develop children's prior knowledge and apply it to new concepts. Prior knowledge can be a useful instructional tool for addressing concepts that might otherwise be especially challenging. Prior knowledge is a combination of children's **beliefs and academic experiences** that affect how students learn. Therefore, it is important for educators to gauge this knowledge in order to plan lessons accordingly. **Know, Want to Know, and Learned charts (KWL)** are useful tools to use before lessons begin. Students explore what they know and want to know about concepts. At the conclusion of the lessons, students examine what they have learned about the concepts. The **Known and Unknown chart strategy** works similarly. Teachers can ask what students know about concepts and write responses down in the known column. What students want to learn more about or do not know goes into the unknown column. Both strategies can be implemented as individual or group activities to introduce lessons.

Guided Learning

Guided learning is practice or instruction completed by the teacher and students together. The goal of **guided learning** is to help students engage in the learning process in order to learn more about how they think and acquire new information. **Guided practice** occurs when the teacher and students complete practice activities together. The advantage of guided practice is that students can

81

learn ways to approach concepts they have just learned. It allows students to understand and ask questions about lesson-related activities before working independently. Guided practice is useful in classrooms for students with and without disabilities because it helps teachers gauge how students learn and what instructional methods work best for them. Additionally, guided practice allows teachers to understand how students are learning the material. It also allows teachers to revisit concepts that are unclear or fine tune any missed lesson objectives.

Diagnostic Prescriptive Method

The diagnostic prescriptive approach to teaching is based on the fact that all students are unique learners. The **diagnostic prescriptive approach** examines factors that impede student learning and how to remedy specific issues. A successful approach begins with a **diagnosis** of what students are bringing to the classroom. This can be completed through careful observations and assessments. Once the skill deficits are clear, **prescriptive teaching** can be put into effect. In this process, teachers examine what will help students the most. It may be switching materials, changing to group settings, or recognizing the need for specialized interventions due to disabilities. In order to address multiple needs in the classroom, lesson plans should be **multi-modal**. Developing strategies in advance to address students' needs is also a highlight of this method. Another important part of this method is evaluating results to determine what was effective or ineffective for entire classes and individual students.

Developmentally Appropriate Math Skills for Young Children

Starting in pre-kindergarten and first grade, children should be able to count to 100, learn how to write numbers, and demonstrate basic addition and subtraction skills. Older students can demonstrate skills associated with counting money and telling time, and they can also understand decimal, place value, and word problem concepts. Students with disabilities may or may not develop what are considered to be **developmentally appropriate mathematics skills** by certain ages or grades. In inclusive special education settings, the needs of these students can be addressed with a number of strategies. **Scaffolding** is the process of breaking down concepts into chunks. Scaffolding addresses the issues that arise when some students are well behind others by allowing students to work at their own pace and helping them connect prior knowledge to new information. This ensures that students have solidified knowledge of concepts before moving on to new concepts.

Teaching Mathematics

Students whose disabilities affect their performances in mathematics require specialized instruction. Eligible students will have Individualized Education Program goals to address their specific needs but are also expected to learn content connected to **state standards**. Additionally, **accommodations and modifications** are available for qualifying students to assist with mathematics instruction. Strategies that can be effective for math instruction for students with disabilities include:

- using the same instructional strategies in all settings, including the home environment and all school environments.
- using concrete objects to teach math concepts, such as using manipulatives to count out number values.
- providing assistive materials, such as calculators and scrap paper.
- explaining and modeling objectives clearly.
- allowing time for students to check their work.

- activating prior knowledge to assist students with learning new concepts.
- providing opportunities for extra tutoring or one-on-one instruction.
- assisting students with self-monitoring their progress.
- encouraging math games to engage learning and interest in math concepts.

Components of Direct Reading Instruction

The purpose of direct learning instruction is to specifically target the needs of students with learning disabilities. **Direct learning instruction** can be provided in many educational settings. Direct instruction breaks concept learning into specific tasks and processes, with focus on mastering one skill before moving onto another skill. With **direct reading instruction**, the key components are teaching phonemic awareness, phonics, fluency, vocabulary development, and comprehension. Effective reading programs address all five areas of reading instruction. **Phonemic awareness** focuses on breaking words into sound units (phonemes). **Phonics** focuses on connecting these sound units with letters (graphemes). Phonics instruction allows students to approach decoding by sounding words out instead of attempting to read the whole words. **Fluency** instruction focuses on teaching students to read unfamiliar words and texts quickly and accurately. **Vocabulary development** helps increase familiarity with frequently occurring words in texts. **Comprehension** instruction focuses on helping students to understand what they have read. In comprehension instruction, learners connect prior knowledge to the texts.

Benefits of the Direct Reading Process

Direct reading instruction is an approach to teaching reading which focuses on specific skill development for early readers. Students frequently enter their schooling years with deficits in reading skills, especially when they are identified as having disabilities. Effective **direct reading programs** include the teaching of phonemic awareness, phonics, fluency, vocabulary development, and comprehension. Teachers are generally trained to implement direct reading programs instead of creating direct instruction curriculum. Specific programs ensure that teachers use the same curriculum and methods in order to effectively implement direct reading instruction. Direct reading instruction and programs are especially helpful for **skill remediation** for at-risk students. Efficient direct reading instruction communicates high standards for learning, is replicable or able to be implemented across a variety of settings, and offers support materials, professional development, and implementation guidance. Direct reading instruction is also proven to be effective for the improvement of reading abilities in at-risk students.

Teaching Social Studies

Depending on their special education classroom placements, students with **disabilities** receive varying degrees of instruction in other core content areas like social studies and science. Students with mild disabilities, such as learning disabilities, likely participate in inclusive classroom settings or general education classroom settings. Depending on a student's grade level, the student may attend a classroom setting with one or two teachers or switch classes and attend settings with many different teachers. Across all settings, students with mild disabilities receive any **accommodations or modifications** explicitly written in their Individualized Education Programs. Students with mild to moderate disabilities may receive instruction in special education classrooms for part or most of the day. In these instances, general education social studies or science classes may not be the most appropriate educational settings. Special educators then teach the content in the special education classrooms, sometimes connecting it with related tasks or skills. Students with moderate disabilities may receive **indirect instruction** in these content areas that is loosely based on content standards and more appropriate for the ways they acquire knowledge.

Teaching Special Education

Special education classrooms, whether inclusive, self-contained, or resource room settings, often need to deliver instruction in **multiple subject areas**. Students in these settings also represent many **levels of learning**. Therefore, one instructional strategy is not always the most effective way to teach students in these settings. In order to provide quality instruction, special educators can place students with similar skill levels into **small groups** during instruction in the content areas. This way, small groups of students can be working on skills that cater to their specific needs. **Classroom centers** are another way to group students. Classroom centers often feature self-guided instruction in skill or content areas where students can work at their own pace. **Rotating centers** allows teachers to instruct groups of students while the other groups work independently on previously learned skills. **Thematic instruction** is a teaching strategy where multiple subject areas are connected and taught within one lesson unit. Themes are effective in special education classrooms because they tie multiple content areas together. Special educators should also provide **multiple levels of materials and books** for student learning to target different learning levels.

Modifying the Stages of Writing to Assist Students with Learning Disabilities

The **writing process** can be especially challenging for new learners but especially for students with disabilities. The writing process can be facilitated by special educators and general educators in order to build adequate writing skills. Teachers must first address the needs of their classes before engaging in the pre-writing stage. Getting to know students provides insight into their prior knowledge and abilities. In the **pre-writing (brainstorming) stage**, teachers help students prepare for the writing process by establishing good content or thinking of things that interest them to write about. In the **writing stage**, students should be taught to write their content using graphic organizers or diagrams that assist with using appropriate formatting, grammar, and punctuation. The **rewriting/revising stage** can be facilitated by providing checklists of errors and having students self-check and revise their own work. In the **editing/proofreading stage**, students can self-check their work or exchange their final written projects with other students or their teachers. This can also be facilitated using formatting checklists and/or grammar and punctuation checklists to monitor the writing process.

Implications of a Mathematics Disability

Disabilities like **dyscalculia** are specific learning disabilities associated with mathematics. Students that have specific learning disabilities in mathematics have trouble with number-related concepts and using symbols or functions. Symptoms of **math disorders** include difficulties with counting numbers, solving math word problems, sequencing events or information, recognizing patterns when adding, subtracting, multiplying or dividing, and understanding concepts associated with time, like days, weeks, seasons, etc. Recalling math facts is also difficult for students with math disabilities. The severity of the disability is impacted when it **coexists** with dyslexia, Attention Deficit Hyperactivity Disorder, anxiety, or other disabilities. Special educators, math tutors, or other professionals can help students with math deficits by providing multi-modal instruction to engage multiple senses and enhance the chances of the students learning the concepts. They may also receive supports according to 504 Plans or Individualized Education Programs that level the educational playing field, such as use of a calculator. Use of concrete examples, visual aids, graph paper, or scratch paper can also assist students with math disabilities.

Teaching Comprehension with Research-Based Reading Intervention Strategies

Comprehension refers to a person's understanding of something. As it pertains to reading, **comprehension** is the understanding of content that has been read. Students with disabilities often struggle with comprehension, which makes teaching **comprehension strategies** essential to their learning. Special educators should teach students to **monitor** their comprehension by being aware of what they have read, identifying what they do not understand, and implementing problem-solving strategies to address what they do not understand. Special educators can also teach students to demonstrate **metacognitive strategies**, such as identifying specifically what they do not understand in texts (i.e. identifying the page numbers or chapters where they are struggling), looking back through the texts to find answers to comprehension questions, rereading sentences or sections they do not understand, and putting sentences they do not understand into their own words. **Graphic organizers**, like story maps and Venn diagrams, also allow students to map out the information they have read by laying out important concepts.

Effects of Deficits in Language Development on the Learning Processes

Without interventions, children with deficits in language development will likely have issues with overall academic success. **Academic success** is inextricably linked with good language development. **Good language development skills** include the ability to understand spoken and written words, as well as literacy skills. When a core knowledge of language is developed in young children, it can be built upon as the children grow and develop during their grade school years. Reading and writing are language-based skills. **Phonological awareness** is an essential skill and key building block for language development. Phonological awareness is a term that refers to students' awareness of sounds, syllables, and words. Students that develop strong phonological skills typically develop good literacy skills. Students with deficits in reading, writing, or math may have difficulties with phonological awareness and miss some building blocks essential for academic success. These deficits generalize to core subject areas as students are required to demonstrate grade-level appropriate skills.

Helping Students with Disabilities Become Solid Emergent Readers

Emergent reading refers to the reading and writing abilities of young readers. They precede **conventional literacy**, which refers to older children's reading and writing behaviors, such as decoding, reading comprehension, oral reading fluency, spelling, and writing. Children with learning disabilities may demonstrate discrepancies between emergent literacy behaviors and conventional literacy behaviors. They may flip-flop between the two stages, showing progress one moment or day and then seeming to forget the next. Educators can foster skills in emergent and conventional reading by teaching **phonological awareness** and **written letter/sound recognition**. These are both baseline skills that affect students' future phonological awareness development. Additionally, educators can provide engaging, age-appropriate activities that facilitate connections between emergent literacy and conventional literacy skills. Activities that promote students' print awareness and knowledge of book conventions also help build solid emergent reader skills.

Transition Process

Collaborating with IEP Team Members

It is important for Individualized Education Program (IEP) team members to **collaborate** with each other in order to certify that students are receiving educational plans that are suitable to their needs in the least restrictive environments. **IEP team members** include special education teachers, general education teachers, parents or legal guardians, students, school district representatives, and others knowledgeable about the students' performances. Each member brings a valuable piece of information about the students for instructional planning and IEP planning meetings. It is important for special educators to establish good relationships and collaborate with the students and parents or legal guardians in order to gauge the students' strengths and weaknesses. Collaboration is essential between the general and special educators in order to ensure that students' IEP goals and needs are being met in the appropriate settings. Collaboration with district team members or others like school psychologists is helpful for gaining insight on special education procedures or assessment results.

Communicating with Related Service Members Across All Special Education Settings

In order to provide the best educations possible for students with disabilities, it is important for special educators and related service members to **communicate** effectively. Communication is important due to the degree of collaboration required between the special educators and the related service members. Related service members are often Individualized Education Program (IEP) team members and help students meet their IEP goals and objectives. **Related service members**, like speech pathologists and occupational therapists, also work on a consultation basis with special educators. They may also consult with general education teachers to ensure that students receive required related services in the general education or inclusive classroom settings. Special educators and related service members must collaborate in order to ensure the needs of the students are met, especially when IEP goals or objectives are out of the scope of the special educators' knowledge bases. For example, a speech pathologist might help a teacher address a student's fluency goal.

Communicating with Parents of Students with Disabilities

It is good practice to communicate with parents outside of progress reporting times and Individualized Education Program meetings. This is especially important for students with **communication deficits** who may not be able to communicate with their parents or legal guardians. Communication also helps prevent potential crises or problem behaviors and alerts parents or legal guardians before any major issues arise. Special educators should find methods of communication that work best for parents or legal guardians, such as phone calls, emails, or writing in daily communication logs. Email is beneficial for creating paper trails, especially for any discussions about educating students. However, email lacks tone and body language and can sometimes be misunderstood. Phone calls fulfill an immediate need to speak with a parent or legal guardian. However, there are no paper trails with phone calls, and they can also lead to misunderstanding. Phone calls may be time consuming, but they can be conducted on special occasions or when behavioral issues need to be discussed. Written communication logs are useful for writing brief summaries about students' days. With any mode of communication, it is essential to **document** what is communicated between the parents or legal guardians and the educators.

Roles of Parents/Legal Guardians and the School District During Evaluation

If parents or legal guardians suspect their children have disabilities, they can request that the school districts **evaluate** the children for special education. A parent or legal guardian can send a **written evaluation request** to the child's school, principal, and the school district's director or director of special education services. In some states, parents and legal guardians may be required to sign a school district form requesting the evaluation. Parents should follow up on the request and/or set a timeframe for the school district to respond. The school district may choose to implement the **Response to Intervention (RTI) pre-referral process**. RTI is a process by which the school gives the student special academic support before determining whether or not to move forward with the evaluation process. Not all states or school districts have the same method for applying RTI. Under IDEA, the timeframe for completion of RTI is 60 days. However, some states can set their own timelines. RTI should not be the only means by which the school district collects data on the student and should be part of a comprehensive evaluation conducted by the student's school.

Speech Language Pathologist

Speech language pathologists (**SLP**) provide interventions for children with communication disorders. They can assist, evaluate, prevent, and diagnose a variety of **speech issues**, from fluency to voice disorders. Before children reach grade school age, it is important that they receive early interventions for suspected communication disorders. SLPs are helpful with targeting speech or language issues, identifying at-risk students, or providing interventions for children and adults. SLPs also play a role in helping children develop good reading and writing skills, especially when deficits are evident. SLPs work collaboratively with special educators to deliver **interventions** to children with speech and language disorders in grade school. In schools, SLPs play a role in prevention, assessment, intervention, program design, data collection and analysis, and Individualized Education Program compliance. SLPs work with special educators, parents, students, reading specialists, occupational therapists, school psychologists, and others in order to provide effective services to students who require them.

Occupational Therapist

Students with special needs may need **occupational therapy services**. The amount of services students receive is defined on their Individualized Education Programs (IEPs). **Occupational therapists (OTs)** may help students on IEPs refine their fine motor skills, improve sensory processing deficits, improve visual skills, and improve self-care skills. OTs can also assist with behavior management, social skills, and improving attention and focus. When a student is identified as possibly needing OT services, the OT spends time observing the student in a variety of settings where the skill or skill deficit will be demonstrated. Prior to the student's IEP meeting, the OT typically meets with the student's teachers, parents, and other professionals in order to discuss observations, assessment results, and determinations. **Determinations** are then put into the IEP and implemented as related services. Fine motor skill instruction begins with the OT instructing the student on a particular skill. OTs can set up regimens for teachers and parents to generalize using the fine motor skills in the classroom and home environments.

Reasonable Accommodations for Students

According to the Americans with Disabilities Act, a **reasonable accommodation** is a change to workplace conditions, equipment, or environment that allow an individual to effectively perform a job. Title I under ADA requires businesses with more than 15 employees to abide by certain regulations, ensuring that their needs are reasonably met. Any change to the work environment or the way a job is performed that gives a person with a disability access to **equal employment** is considered a reasonable accommodation. Reasonable accommodations fall into **three categories**: changes to a job application process, changes to the work environment or to the way a job is usually done, and changes that enable employee access to equal benefits and privileges that employees without disabilities receive. These effectively level the playing field for people with disabilities to receive the same benefits as their peers. It also allows for the fewest barriers to success in the workplace. Many communities have resources available to help people with disabilities find jobs. They also have resources that help employers make their workplaces accessible for people with disabilities.

Paraprofessional

The U.S. Department of Education requires **paraprofessionals** to have high school diplomas or equivalent under Title 1 law. Paraprofessionals (paras), sometimes called **paraeducators**, assist classroom teachers with classroom activities and help students with special needs. In a special education setting, a para works with a certified teacher to help deliver **instruction** and help students meet **Individualized Education Program goals and objectives**. Paras are not responsible for teaching new skills or introducing new goals and objectives to students. In this respect, special educators generally work alongside the paras and students to introduce new skills, goals, or objectives. At times, paras may be responsible for helping students maintain behavior plans, working with students who may be aggressive or violent, and providing physical assistance if necessary. Training is usually provided by the school district for situations when physical assistance is a possible necessity. Paras can also help take notes on students' progress toward meeting their goals or objectives. They can also discuss how students are progressing with behavior plans.

Teaching Strategies and Accommodations for Students with Working Memory Deficits

Working memory is critical for remembering letters and numbers, listening to short instructions, reading and understanding content, completing homework independently, and understanding social cues. When **working memory skills** are absent or slow to develop, learning may be difficult. This may get worse for children over time. As they fail to develop or retain working memory capabilities, their overall **cognitive abilities** begin to suffer. Working memory deficits differ from person to person with disabilities, but accommodations can be made to make up for missing or developing skills. Educators can implement **strategies** like reducing the children's workload, providing visual cues, being aware of when children might be reaching memory overload, providing positive feedback, providing testing alternatives, and providing extra time. **Accommodations** on an Individualized Education Program for a student with working memory deficits might include frequent breaks, small group instruction, and extended time for tests and assignments.

Classroom Accommodations That Allow Students with Disabilities to Be Successful

Accommodations are flexible classroom tools because they can be used to provide **interventions** without time or location boundaries. They remove **barriers** to learning for students with disabilities, and they change how students learn. Accommodations do not change what the students are learning or expected to know. Classroom accommodations may be outlined in students' Individualized Education Programs or 504 Plans, or simply provided on the spot by the special educators or general educators. Accommodations are put into place to ensure that the students with disabilities are accessing the learning process with the fewest barriers, putting them on the same levels as their peers without disabilities. **Presentation accommodations** include allowing students to listen to instructions orally, providing written lists of instructions, and allowing students to use readers to assist with comprehension. **Response accommodations** include allowing students to provide oral responses, capture responses via audio recording, and/or use spelling dictionaries or spell checkers when writing. **Accommodations to setting** include special seating (wherever the students learn best), use of sensory tools, and/or use of special lighting.

Effect of Home Life Factors on Learning and Development

Students' home lives are interconnected with their school lives. **Home and life factors**, especially negative ones, are difficult for students to avoid generalizing to the school environment. **Home stressors** can often develop into dysfunction at school for children with disabilities. Factors that affect the learning and development of students with disabilities include academic factors, environmental factors, intellectual factors, language factors, medical factors, perceptual factors, and psychological factors. **Academic factors** include developmental delays in core content areas, lack of basic skills, and apparent inconsistency of learning in certain stages of development. **Environmental factors** occur when children are exposed to home life trauma, such as divorce, drug abuse, alcoholism, parental fighting, or family illness. **Intellectual factors** include limited intellectual abilities or unnoticed gifted abilities. **Language factors** include issues with language barriers or language acquisition, such as aphasia, bilingualism, expressive language disorder, or pragmatic language disorder. **Medical factors** include Attention Deficit Hyperactivity Disorder, muscular problems, or hearing problems. **Perceptual factors** include any factors that affect or slow down students' processing of information. **Psychological factors** include depression, anxiety, or conduct disorders.

Social Skill Deficits That Occur in Students with Disabilities

Social skills are a concept that needs to be taught to some students with disabilities, such as students with autism. **Social skills instruction** involves the teaching of basic communication skills, empathy and rapport skills, interpersonal skills, problem-solving skills, and accountability. **Basic communication skills** include listening skills, following directions, and avoiding speaking out of turn. **Empathy and rapport skills** involve teaching students how to demonstrate empathy and build rapport. **Interpersonal skills** must be learned by teaching students to demonstrate skills like sharing, joining activities, and participating in turn taking. **Problem-solving skills** sometimes need to be taught as well. These include teaching students to ask for help, apologize to others, make decisions, and accept consequences. **Accountability** must be taught to students so they can learn to follow through on promises and accept criticisms appropriately. These are skills that do not come naturally to students with social skill deficits.

Obtaining Accommodations in the Classroom Setting

When parents or legal guardians of children with disabilities believe that **accommodations** may help their children, they can arrange to speak with the teachers about informal supports. **Informal supports** are strategies the teachers can put into place to assist the students with their learning processes. These changes do not require paperwork and can be provided during classroom instruction. Teachers can experiment with informal supports to determine what will be most helpful for removing the barriers to learning the students might be experiencing. If it is determined that students need bigger changes to how they learn, **formal evaluations** can take place. If the students are not already on Individualized Education Programs or 504 Plans, these needs may lead to initial evaluations to collect data on the students' needs. For students with IEPs or 504 Plans, accommodations that help the students can be included on their next IEPs or 504 Plans. The IEPs or 504 Plans can also be **amended** if the need for the accommodations is immediate, such as if they need to be put in place before standardized testing time. In both situations, **data** supporting the need for the accommodations must be provided and listed in the comprehensive initial evaluations, initial IEPs or 504 Plans, or the students' amended IEPs or 504 Plans.

Informal Supports vs. Formal Accommodations

Informal supports are generally easier to implement in the classroom setting. They do not necessarily have to be implemented only for students on Individualized Education Programs or students with disabilities. Students who have not been evaluated for special education services can receive **informal supports** to ensure classroom success. When teachers see students struggling with the ways they are learning, the teachers may use informal supports to help the students. They may demonstrate that the students are able to learn with the accommodations in place. Informal supports are often the first step to indicating that students are in need of **special education services**. **Formal accommodations** come into place when students become eligible for IEPs or 504 Plans. Formal supports are written into the IEPs or 504 Plans and then required by law to be provided. Examples of informal supports include frequent breaks, special seating, quiet areas for test taking or studying, teacher cues, and help with basic organizational skills. These informal supports may eventually turn into formal supports if and when students become eligible for special education services.

Inclusion Classroom Setting

The Individuals with Disabilities Education Act does not expressly define a **least restrictive environment** for each specific disability. Typically, it is up to the Individualized Education Program team of professionals, including the student's parent or legal guardian, to determine the best case **LRE setting** possible for an individual student. Mainstreaming is a term that is often used interchangeably with inclusion. A **mainstreaming or inclusion setting** means the student with a disability is included in the general education setting the entire school day. The student may receive supports and services like an aide, related services, assistive technology, accommodations, or modifications that are appropriate for the individual student. These supports and services seek to help the student with a disability gain access to the general education curriculum with the fewest barriers. This model essentially seeks to level the playing field for the student with a disability so that he or she may learn alongside general education peers. For these students, the LRE setting must be justified in the Individualized Education Program.

Self-Contained Classroom Setting

The Individuals with Disabilities Education Act states that according to least restrictive environment standards, students in an LRE are ideally spending as much time as possible with their non-disabled peers in the **general education setting**. IDEA states that LRE means a student should receive general education "to the maximum extent that is appropriate," and that special classes, special schools, or removal from the general education classroom should only happen when a child's needs are greater than what can be provided by supplementary aids and services. A **self-contained classroom setting** can be a separate class of students within a school or a separate school that specifically addresses the needs of children with disabilities. In both settings, the needs of the students are greater than what can be offered in the general education classroom, even with educational supports. Settings like these may be specialized in instruction and support for students with similar needs. For these children, their placements in self-contained classrooms must be justified on their Individualized Education Programs.

Partial Mainstream/Inclusion Classroom Setting

It is generally up to the Individualized Education Program team of professionals and the student's parent or legal guardian to determine a least restrictive environment that best suits the needs of the student. In a **partial mainstream/inclusion classroom setting**, a student spends part of the day in the **general education classroom**. The student receives part of his or her education in a separate, **special education classroom**. This type of LRE is determined when a student's needs are greater than what services can be provided in the general education classroom, even with educational supports or services in place. For example, a student with severe deficits in mathematical skills may be placed in a classroom outside the general education classroom that targets specific needs and skills. The student may also get pulled out of the general education classroom to receive one-on-one instruction or small group instruction. For these children, their placements in partial mainstream/inclusion classrooms must be justified on their Individualized Education Programs.

Specialized Educational Settings

School districts sometimes offer specialized educational settings for students with disabilities, such as **special preschools**. Preschools for children with disabilities typically focus on children ages 3–5. They are important resources for teaching early learning, communication, and social skills that are essential for children with disabilities. **Life skills settings** are where students with disabilities can receive specialized instruction in academic, social, behavioral, or daily living skills. **Social behavior skills settings** are sometimes called applied behavior skills or behavior skills. In this type of setting, the primary focus is on social and decision-making skills. **Transition settings** are available for students making the transition from high school to life after high school. Students with Individualized Education Programs can stay in high school until the age of 21 or 22, depending on the calendar month they turn 22. Transition settings assist students with work experiences, post-secondary education experiences, and independent living skills.

Parents/Legal Guardians Ensuring Accommodations Are Being Provided

Accommodations are changes to the ways children with disabilities learn, not changes to what the children are learning. Parents can ensure that accommodations are being provided in a number of ways. Unless specifically stated on the students' Individualized Education Programs or 504 Plans, parents and legal guardians may only receive **formal updates** on how accommodations are being provided or helping the students during specified reporting times. However, parents and legal guardians can ask for **reports** on goal progress or accommodations for their students at any time. Parents and legal guardians can ensure that accommodations are successfully implemented by using the schools' progress reports and by asking the right questions. Parents and legal guardians can **advocate** for their students' accommodations by making sure the accommodations are being implemented on a regular basis. Parents and legal guardians also have the right to ask if students are using the accommodations on a **regular basis**. If they are being used on a regular basis, parents and legal guardians can explore options that might also help the students. Parents and legal guardians can work with the special education teachers and/or the IEP teams to ensure that their students' accommodations are being received and are effective.

Evaluating, Modifying, and Adapting the Classroom Setting Using the UDL

The **Universal Design for Learning (UDL) model** is most successful when the classroom teacher prepares a classroom setting that encourages the success of students with and without disabilities. Knowledge of the **characteristics** of students with different disabilities, as well as the unique

learning needs of these students, ensures that the classroom teacher is aware of and addresses these needs in the classroom setting. Setting clear short and/or long-term goals for students to achieve is one way to meet the UDL standards. A traditional classroom may offer one assignment for all students to complete, but a UDL compliant classroom may offer **different assignments** or **different ways** for students to complete the assignment. UDL compliant classrooms also offer **flexible workspaces** for the students to complete their classwork. Students may have access to quiet spaces for individual work or group tables for group work. Students in a UDL compliant classroom also receive regular **feedback** throughout their classwork rather than receiving one grade upon assignment completion. UDL compliant teachers recognize that students access information differently and provide different ways for students to gain **access**, such as audio text.

Evaluating, Modifying, and Adapting the Classroom Curriculum Using the UDL

In order for a **Universal Design for Learning (UDL) model classroom** to be successful, the classroom teacher must evaluate, modify, and adapt the classroom **curriculum** to best suit the needs of the individual students. UDL contrasts with a one-size-fits-all concept of curriculum planning, where lesson plans are developed and implemented strictly based on how teachers expect students to learn. Instead, a successful UDL model addresses the many **specific needs** of a classroom of students. These needs may vary depending on the unique abilities each classroom of students presents. UDL compliant teachers can evaluate the success of lessons by checking the achievement of students using **formal and informal assessments**. UDL compliant teachers utilize these assessments throughout the lessons, instead of upon lesson completion. These teachers use the results of the evaluations to modify and/or adapt classroom instruction to best meet the needs of the students. Evaluation methods given informally can provide a lot of information about whether or not students are grasping the concepts. UDL compliant teachers use evaluation results to reflect upon lessons and determine how to move forward with future lessons.

Evaluating, Modifying, and Adapting the Classroom Materials and Equipment Using the UDL

In order for a **Universal Design for Learning (UDL) classroom** to be successful, the classroom teacher must evaluate, modify, and adapt the classroom **materials and equipment** to best suit the needs of the individual students. When teachers are **UDL compliant**, they are observing the needs of the students and making necessary changes to materials and/or equipment to ensure student success. A way for teachers to determine the success of classroom materials or equipment is through **formal and informal assessments**. Informal assessments in particular are helpful for receiving immediate feedback as to whether materials are appropriate for student learning. A UDL compliant teacher may offer multiple ways for students to present what they learned, instead of completing pencil and paper assignments. **Multiple assignment completion options** ensure that the unique abilities of students are being targeted, instead of just targeting one or two specific skills. **Equipment** such as audio or digital text, when paired with words, can assist students who have issues with listening or comprehension. A UDL compliant teacher may choose to pair audio output and text during a reading assignment for all students in order to target students with listening or comprehension difficulties.

Principles of the Universal Design for Learning Model

The UDL model contains three principles that aim to level the playing field for all learners. **Principle I** of the Universal Design for Learning model primarily focuses on what **representation or version** of information is being taught. This principle aims to target an audience of diverse learners. By providing multiple ways for students to approach content, teachers can ensure that the unique needs of all learners in their classrooms are met. **Principle II** examines the how of learning.

This principle focuses on the concept that students learn best when provided with **multiple ways** to demonstrate what they have learned. In Principle II compliant classrooms, students are given more than one option for expressing themselves. **Principle III** maintains a focus on providing multiple ways for students to engage in the learning process. Principle III compliant teachers provide options for keeping content **interesting and relevant** to all types of learners. In effective UDL model classrooms, these principles are generally met by providing multiple ways to learn the content, express what was learned, and engage in lesson content.

Implementing Modifications and Accommodations in an Inclusive Classroom Setting

General educators can work with special educators to create an effective **co-teaching model**. In an effective co-teaching model, both the general educator and special educator demonstrate the **Universal Design for Learning Framework**. This ensures that the needs of the diverse group of learners are being met. For students using Individualized Education Programs, modifications such as reduced work would be expressly written in their IEPs. In a co-teaching model, student modifications would be communicated to the **general educator**. The **special educator** can work with the general educator to provide the modifications in the inclusive classroom setting. Students using IEPs may have accommodations expressly written in their IEPs. These accommodations may or may not be used in an **inclusive setting**, depending on the relevancy of the accommodation. For example, the accommodation of using a calculator would be utilized in a math class but not a social studies class. In addition to expressly written accommodations, special educators and general educators can work together in the setting to provide appropriate **accommodations** during the learning process. These types of accommodations may be part of informal assessments used to adjust instruction.

Role of Paraeducators

Paraeducators, sometimes referred to as aides or paraprofessionals, are part of students' educational teams. **Paraeducators** work under the supervision of special educators or principals and are key contributors to the learning process for certain students. Their primary role, especially if their positions are funded by the Individuals with Disabilities Education Act, is to provide **educational support** for students. For students using Individualized Education Programs, the use of paraeducators is typically included in the IEPs. Paraeducators can facilitate the learning process for students by removing learning barriers, keeping track of goal progress, or organizing goal-tracking activities. Paraeducators cannot introduce new concepts or take over the role of highly qualified teachers. Paraeducators cannot make changes to what students are learning, unless specific modifications are listed in the students' IEPs. They cannot provide accommodations unless the accommodations are appropriate for what is written in the students' IEPs. The paraeducators may also be instructed by supervising teachers or principals to facilitate and monitor accommodations or modifications for students and reinforce learned concepts.

Benefits of Collaborative Teaching and the Co-Teaching Model

If determined by an Individualized Education Program (IEP), a student with a disability may participate in an **inclusive setting**. In some classrooms, students participate in **co-taught settings**. In this **collaborative teaching environment**, the general educator and special educator work together to meet the goals of the students with disabilities in the regular education classroom. Students in this setting are all taught to the same educational standards. However, accommodations and modifications may be implemented for students with disabilities. In a successful collaborative teaching model, the special educator and general educator may cooperatively implement the accommodations and modifications for these students. A two-teacher setting also gives students more opportunities to receive individualized instruction, work in small groups, or receive one-on-one attention. Collaborative teaching in the co-taught setting can facilitate differentiated instruction, help the teachers meet the Universal Design for Learning framework, and provide individualized learning opportunities.

Fostering the Communication Development of Students with ASD

Students with **Autism Spectrum Disorder** (ASD) vary in their need for communication and social skill assistance and instruction. Some students with ASD may demonstrate slight to extreme delays in language, difficulty sustaining conversations, and the inability to understand body language, tone of voice, and facial expressions. Since ASD is a **spectrum disorder**, there typically is no single instructional strategy or technique that works for all students with the disorder. Some **evidence-based strategies** are effective for teaching appropriate communication skills to students with ASD. **Applied behavioral analysis (ABA)** is an evidence-based strategy that involves providing an intervention and analyzing its effectiveness for a student with ASD. **Discrete trial training (DTT)** is a teaching strategy that is more structured than ABA. It focuses on teaching and reinforcing skills in smaller increments. **Pivotal response treatment (PRT)** is an ABA-derived approach that focuses more on meaningful reinforcement when general behaviors occur. PRT targets progress in areas of development rather than focusing on decreasing specific behaviors.

Managing Distractions That May Affect Learning and Development

Managing distractions is a part of good teaching practices. Special educators demonstrate good **classroom management strategies** when they:

- create positive learning environments by getting to know students' individual emotional, intellectual, social, and physical needs.
- remove or accommodate environmental triggers specific to students.
- remove or accommodate behavioral triggers.
- encourage students to help with classroom jobs and small tasks.
- create preemptive lesson plans for anticipated behaviors.
- attempt verbal de-escalation first when behavioral issues arise.
- set clear, consistent rules.
- set and follow through with consequences for breaking the rules.
- take time to get to know students and their triggers.
- create seating arrangements that minimize distractions.
- teach social skills, thinking skills, test-taking skills, problem-solving skills, and self-regulation skills alongside academic content.
- use visual aids in lessons.
- utilize peer-instructional opportunities.
- provide opportunities for breaks.
- incorporate computer-based programs, which can hold the attention of students with disabilities like autism.

Strategies for Planning, Implementing, and Facilitating Intrinsic Motivation

Intrinsic motivation is a person's inner drive to engage in an activity or behavior. Students with special needs often struggle with intrinsic motivation as a skill. This requires special educators and other professionals to promote and/or teach students to be intrinsically motivated. Teachers can **promote intrinsic motivation** by giving students opportunities to demonstrate **achievement**. This can be done by challenging students with intellectual risks and helping them focus on challenging classwork or tasks. Teachers should also build upon students' strengths by providing daily opportunities in the classroom for students to demonstrate their **strengths** instead of focusing on their weaknesses. Offering choices throughout the day provides students with ownership of their decision-making and communicates that they have choices in the classroom environment. Teachers should also allow students to **fail without criticism** and instead promote self-reflection in order to build students' confidence. Teachers should also instruct students on how to **break down tasks** and promote other self-management skills and organizational skills.

Instructional Methods for Teaching Students with Social Skills Deficits

Students with social skills deficits often need instruction in social skill areas. These deficits can be addressed in inclusive settings and may not necessarily require explicit social skills instruction. **Social skills instruction** can be delivered to entire classes or individual students, depending on the needs of the students. Students will sometimes also receive **one-on-one** or **small group social skills instruction** from professionals like speech-language pathologists, especially when this is written in students' Individualized Education Programs (IEPs). In these situations, the idea is for the students to generalize learned concepts to their school and home environments. In both settings, it is important to model appropriate manners, hold students responsible for their actions, and have clear and concise rules and consequences. This solidifies educational environments that are both predictable and safe. Social situations that produce undesired outcomes can be remediated by **role-playing** the situations and teaching students positive responses. **Social stories** are another way to foster social skills growth. Often, these social stories demonstrate how people should respond to specific social situations appropriately.

Promoting Learning and Development

Educators that practice effective strategies for **promoting learning and development** create successful learning environments and help struggling learners. Teachers should take the time to know the **strengths and weaknesses** of individual students in order to plan and implement instructional matches, including curriculum that challenges students without frustrating them. **Scaffolding** is a strategy that breaks larger concepts into smaller chunks. This process helps students learn new concepts and apply prior knowledge. Instruction should be broken up into step-by-step strategies in order to allow students to follow steps or remediate certain concepts. **Modeling and demonstrating** tasks or lessons is useful for demonstrating problem-solving abilities. Students mastering new content should also receive consistent, positive **feedback** for their achievements. Additionally, students should be given opportunities to **talk through their processes** with peers or in teacher-led groups when learning new concepts.

Selecting Developmentally Appropriate Curriculum

Choosing a developmentally appropriate curriculum is challenging for educators. Special educators have the additional challenge of finding a curriculum that meets the needs of the **individual students with disabilities**. The end result is not usually a one-size-fits-all curriculum because that goes against the intentions of individualized education programs that meet the needs of students with special needs. Instead, special educators often pick and choose curriculum components that best meet the needs of differing abilities in the classroom. When selecting appropriate curriculum, special educators should consider:

- standards and goals that are appropriate to the needs of the classroom students.
- best practices that have been found effective for classroom students.
- curriculum that is engaging and challenging.

- instruction and activities that are multi-modal.
- Individualized Education Program (IEP) goals.
- real-world experiences.
- different ways of learning that help teachers understand students' learning processes.
- collaboration with co-teachers to deliver appropriate instruction.

In some special education settings, the curriculum is already chosen. In these settings, teachers can collaborate with co-teachers to find ways to provide instruction that meets standards and the individual needs of the classroom students.

Accessibility Components of a Picture Exchange Communication System

A Picture Exchange Communication System (**PECS**) is a communication system for people with little or no **communicative abilities**. This system is a way for the students to access their environments using a unique communication system. PECS is a way for people with limited communicative abilities to use **picture symbols** to communicate meaning, wants, and needs. Children can learn a PECS system by using pictures to request and receive items. For example, a child may point to a picture symbol to request a book. PECS is a way for students with communication disorders to develop their **verbal communication** without actually speaking. It eliminates frustration and problem behaviors by providing students with an avenue to express what they want to say. It is commonly used for students with Autism Spectrum disorder in the form of augmentative communication devices. It can also be used for students with other impairments whose communicative abilities are affected. PECS focuses on **functional communication skills** and can be practiced in the home, school, and community environments.

Using Visual Supports to Facilitate Instruction and Self-Monitoring Strategies

Many students learn best when provided with instruction and activities that appeal to multiple senses. A **multi-modal approach** is especially important for students with developmental disabilities who may need supports that meet their individual ways of learning. **Visual supports** are concrete representations of information used to convey meaning. Visual supports can be used by teachers of students with developmental disabilities to help them understand what is being taught and communicated to them. Visual supports can help students with understanding classroom rules, making decisions, communicating with others, staying organized, and reducing frustrations. **Visual schedules** show students visual representations of their daily schedules. This assists with transitions between activities, which can sometimes be difficult for students with disabilities. Visuals can be used to help students share information about themselves or their school days with their peers and parents. Visual supports can also be used with checklists to help facilitate independence, and behavior checklists can be used to help students self-monitor their behaviors.

Using Instructional Methods to Address Independent Living Skills

When applicable, goals for independent living skills are included in the **transition section** of students' Individualized Education Plans. However, **independent living skills education** should begin well before students reach high school, regardless of whether or not these skills are addressed in their IEP goals. **Functional skills instruction** is necessary to teach students skills needed to gain independence. Instructional methods used to address independent living skills for students with disabilities include making life skills instruction part of the daily curriculum. An appropriate **task analysis** can be used to determine what skills need to be taught. **Functional academic skills**, especially in the areas of math and language arts, should also be included in the curriculum. Basic skills like telling time, balancing a bank account, and recognizing signs and symbols are just some examples of skills that students can generalize outside of the classroom environment. The goal of **community-based instruction** is to help students develop skills needed to succeed in the community, such as skills needed when riding a bus or shopping. This type of instruction may be harder to implement than basic social skills training, which should take place in the daily curriculum.

58

FTCE Practice Test

1. What was the first major federal law guaranteeing all children aged 5-21 the right to a public education?
    a. IDEA
    b. EHA
    c. FAPE
    d. LRE

2. According to the law's procedural safeguards, who can request a due process hearing regarding the identification, evaluation, placement, or provision of education to a child with a disability?
    a. The child's parents
    b. The parents or the school
    c. The parents' attorney
    d. All of the above

3. Relative to public schools, the basic legal and ethical principles on which both FERPA and the student record Privacy Rule of HIPAA were founded…
    a. Are completely unrelated
    b. Overlap in some areas
    c. Are the same principles
    d. Differ in important ways

4. In the IEP process, which of the following takes place first?
    a. evaluation
    b. identification
    c. eligibility
    d. meeting

5. During which step of the IEP process are classroom accommodations and modifications tested for effectiveness?
    a. Identification
    b. Pre-referral
    c. Eligibility
    d. Review

6. Under current IDEA regulations, which of the following can determine that a child has a disability?
    a. Lack of appropriate instruction in reading
    b. Lack of appropriate teaching in mathematics
    c. Lack of proficiency in the English language
    d. None of the above

7. The most recent amendments to the IDEA include which provision regarding the identification of specific learning disabilities?
    a. Requiring a severe discrepancy between competence and performance is prohibited
    b. Identifying a severe discrepancy between competence and performance is mandatory
    c. Establishing that a student's competence and performance are comparable is required
    d. These amendments do not address comparison between competence and performance

8. Compared to a child with normal development, a child with spina bifida would be *most* likely to demonstrate deficits in...

   a. Intellectual development
   b. Language development
   c. Motor development
   d. Social development

9. Among the following, a child with which type of disability is likely to be best at focusing attention on one thing for a long time?

   a. Down syndrome
   b. Developmental delay
   c. Attention deficit disorder
   d. Autism spectrum disorder

10. Which of the following are children born with rubella NOT more likely to have?

   a. Deafness
   b. Paralysis
   c. Blindness
   d. Cataracts

11. A major review of an exceptional student's IEP is required...

   a. Once every year
   b. Once every three years
   c. In one or three years by state
   d. In varying periods by each state

12. The school psychologist is explaining assessment results to Clifford's parents and other IEP team members. She says that Clifford has difficulties with planning, organizing, keeping track of time, relating a current lesson to earlier learning, and that he talks out of turn in class. These all relate most to deficits in...

   a. Executive function
   b. Self-regulation
   c. Sequencing
   d. Memory

13. In an IEP meeting, who is the best choice to interpret a student's evaluation results?

   a. Whoever can best explain the educational implications of those results
   b. The student's special education teacher on the IEP team
   c. The school psychologist who may or may not be an IEP team member
   d. Another professional who is not a part of the student's IEP team

14. Which of the following models used in planning instruction for students with disabilities is described as an example of "student-directed planning"?

   a. The model and process of Group Action Planning (GAP)
   b. The Choosing Options and Accommodations for Children (COACH) model
   c. The model and process of Making Action Plans (MAPs)
   d. The Planning Alternative Tomorrows with Hope (PATH) model

15. Which of the following is an independent federal agency that makes recommendations to both the President and Congress regarding issues related to disabilities?

   a. Federation for Children with Special Needs (FCSN)
   b. Center for Personal Assistance Services (CPAS)
   c. National Disability Rights Network (NDRN)
   d. The National Council on Disability (NCD)

16. What is the *primary* purpose of universal newborn hearing screenings?

   a. Educational planning
   b. Disability diagnosis
   c. Early identification
   d. IDEA eligibility

17. The type of assessment most often used to evaluate the effectiveness of instruction is a(n)...

   a. Authentic assessment
   b. Ongoing assessment
   c. Formative assessment
   d. Summative assessment

18. In conducting assessments appropriate to the needs of students with disabilities, what is NOT a provision of the 2004 IDEA reauthorization?

   a. A number of different assessment instruments and methods should be used
   b. Assessment information should be used to determine if a child has a disability
   c. Altering test language compromises test validity and thus should be avoided
   d. Physical, developmental, cognitive, and behavioral factors should be assessed

19. Which of the following is most congruent with general ethical principles regarding assessment information?

   a. Informally disclosing student test results to members of school faculty or staff
   b. Breaking confidentiality in cases of obvious danger to an individual or to society
   c. Making formal reports of students' assessment results before parent consent
   d. Assessing culturally diverse students regardless of lack of cultural competence

20. Comparing a student's performance on a test to a national average for age/grade level is a(n)...

   a. Norm-referenced test
   b. Criterion-referenced test
   c. Performance-based test
   d. Ipsative measure/test

21. Which of the following is true regarding these forms of assessment?

   a. Criterion-referenced tests tend to promote competition among students
   b. Norm-referenced tests are good for assessing instructional effectiveness
   c. Criterion-referenced tests foster cooperation and are oriented to success
   d. Norm-referenced tests can be used to aid in individual student diagnoses

22. Jim has mild cognitive impairment. On annual standardized tests, his scores averaged 20 percent below national averages this year and 35 percent below last year. He scored 90 percent correct on his performance-based assessments. He has met or exceeded his IEP goals to increase his criterion-referenced classroom test scores by an average of 10 percent over last year. Based on this information, which of the following is correct?

    a. Jim's instruction is effective because he is demonstrating progress and meeting goals
    b. Jim's instruction is not effective enough because he scored well below national norms
    c. Jim's instruction is effective within the school, but needs work for standardized tests
    d. Jim's instruction may or may not be effective; more information is needed to decide

23. What kind of assessment instrument is most likely to show a normal distribution?

    a. A criterion-referenced measure
    b. A norm-referenced instrument
    c. A performance-based measure
    d. A portfolio assessment measure

24. For portfolio assessments, when a teacher evaluates a young student's portfolio, which type of evaluation typically produces several scores?

    a. Narrative evaluation
    b. General impression scoring
    c. Focused holistic scoring
    d. Analytical scoring

25. Keith has a behavior disorder and expressive language deficits. His teacher wants to evaluate his progress toward his IEP goals for behavior. Which of the following would be the most appropriate method?

    a. Norm-referenced testing
    b. The teacher interviews Keith
    c. Observational assessment
    d. Curriculum-based testing

26. In 2005, how likely was it for African-American and Native American students to receive special education services under the IDEA as it was for students from all other racial/ethnic groups combined?

    a. Half as likely
    b. Twice as likely
    c. 3.2 times as likely
    d. 1.5 times as likely

27. The most recent government data show specific learning disabilities as the largest disability category of students aged 6-21 receiving special education services under the IDEA. Which of the following ranks the next four largest categories in order from most to least?

    a. Speech-language impairments, other health impairments, intellectual disabilities, emotional disturbance

    b. Other health impairments, emotional disturbance, intellectual disabilities, speech-language impairments

    c. Intellectual disabilities, speech-language impairments, emotional disturbance, other health impairments

    d. Emotional disturbance, intellectual disabilities, other health impairments, speech-language impairments

28. When African-American elementary school students in low-income urban backgrounds were given a standardized IQ test, one question asked them to match the word "cup" with one of multiple choices like "saucer," "table," "chair," etc., with "saucer" deemed the correct choice. A large proportion of these children chose "table." This choice is best attributed to...

    a. Cultural and intellectual deprivation at home

    b. Group socioeconomic and cultural differences

    c. Lack of appropriate instruction caused by biases

    d. Lack of understanding from language differences

29. For students with IEP goals to improve auditory comprehension, which of the following is the best assessment method to monitor their progress?

    a. Retelling a story they heard

    b. Informal reading inventory

    c. Curriculum-based testing

    d. Periodic fluency checking

30. In scientifically based research, if data are found to be valid, this means that...

    a. The measurements can be repeated with consistent results

    b. Everybody in the research community agrees the data are right

    c. The measurements measure what they purport to measure

    d. The measurements are for answering significant questions

31. The term reliability in scientifically based research means that a measurement...

    a. Measures or tests what it is meant to measure or test

    b. Can be replicated many times with consistent findings

    c. Is trustworthy by being based on a body of prior study

    d. Has been proven by being used before for many years

32. Which of the following statements is correct regarding features of scientifically based research?

    a. Its main features differ among fields like education, medicine, psychology, etc.

    b. It is used to address whatever question(s) most interest individual researchers

    c. Reputable journals do not find peer review to be a prerequisite for publication

    d. The researchers must consider potential alternate reasons for their conclusions

33. What strategy listed here is most designed to promote generalization of learning?

    a. Having a student practice a new skill in a variety of different settings/contexts
    b. Having a student practice a new skill regularly and periodically testing that skill
    c. Having a student practice a complex skill one step at a time, then adding steps
    d. Having a student practice a new skill in class before applying it in real-life tasks

34. Which of the following is true regarding alternate curriculum programs?

    a. These programs are the first choice for students identified with disabilities
    b. A student's eligibility for these programs is determined by his/her IEP team
    c. They are preferable to general curricula with accommodations/modifications
    d. Students are still assigned to general education classrooms in these programs

35. General education teachers are specialists in curriculum content. What are special education teachers' specialists in?

    a. Assessment
    b. Adaptations
    c. A and B
    d. None of the above

36. Which of the following does Vygotsky's term "scaffolding" refer to?

    a. A structural framework that a teacher creates for a lesson
    b. Support that is always present for a child with special needs
    c. An organizational structure that guides social interactions
    d. Support that is gradually withdrawn as independence grows

37. Albert Bandura's research found that observation of modeling...

    a. Can never produce results like hands-on learning
    b. Will work in real life but not from viewing video
    c. Can have an impact equal to firsthand experience
    d. Improves skill learning but doesn't affect behavior

38. Which of the following is correct about classroom modifications for students with disabilities?

    a. Teachers rarely make incidental adaptations to address immediate problems
    b. Comprehensive plans for students with disabilities should include adaptations
    c. Classroom modifications made on the spot are unnecessary and inappropriate
    d. Teachers' intentional, planned adaptations are unlikely to meet student needs

39. Which of the following is most accurate regarding textbooks that elementary school teachers use when teaching culturally diverse students?

    a. Textbooks introduce many new concepts in a short time for such students
    b. Teacher editions commonly offer tips for meeting diverse students' needs
    c. The reading levels of most textbooks are appropriate for diverse students
    d. Most textbooks eliminate the need for much differentiation of instruction

40. In teaching basic mathematics, the following actions by teachers will benefit all students. However, which one is most likely to be needed more specifically for students with special needs in a general education classroom?

    a. Carefully planning the coverage and order of instructional math content
    b. Judicious selection and application of the specific instructional strategies
    c. Designing practice activities that take student special needs into account
    d. Giving intensive, direct instruction in mathematics to individual students

41. TeacherVision (a part of Family Education Network), partnering with the Council for Exceptional Children, provides a Planning Pyramid to help teachers plan lessons for special needs and diverse students. Which of the following is true about the purposes of this tool?

    a. It keeps teachers from having unrealistic expectations of such students
    b. It enables educators to place such students in appropriate school tracks
    c. It permits all of the students to have equal access to all of the information
    d. It provides a way to dictate the sequence in which all students will learn

42. Which of the following is the most efficient *and* effective method for teaching word recognition to a class with a variety of student levels and needs?

    a. Individual direct instructions
    b. Multilevel teaching practices
    c. Teaching to the class median
    d. Smaller groups at each level

43. Which of the following is most accurate regarding grouping strategies for teaching disabled and diverse students using multilevel instructional techniques?

    a. These are best taught to the whole class
    b. Small groups are the optimal arrangement
    c. Multilevel instruction is best used in pairs
    d. A range of grouping strategies can be used

44. Which of the following statements is most true about adaptations teachers may need to use in testing, teaching, and materials to address the needs of individual students?

    a. Some students use communication modes unfamiliar to the teacher
    b. Differentiation of instruction is unnecessary between boys and girls
    c. Teachers are unlikely to encounter age differences in the same class
    d. Students speaking other languages must quickly adapt to using English

45. Which of the following is most accurate about what teachers need to consider in planning lessons in reading and math for both special needs students and the class as a whole?

    a. They already know which skill or concept they want to teach
    b. They assume students have prerequisites for a skill/concept
    c. They must determine what mastery of a skill/concept requires
    d. They are premature in thinking how to expand/apply learning

46. Mr. Stewart's students show good reading comprehension of any given paragraph in any chapter of their textbook, but they have trouble organizing, recalling, or applying the main points of a chapter. Which of the following is the simplest, most direct and efficient way to help?

    a. Point out and explain the text's informational structure and features
    b. Create separate handouts with simplified organization of main points
    c. Identify, select, procure, duplicate, and distribute graphic organizers
    d. Create and deliver a Power Point® presentation for each text chapter

47. Which of the following is the most accurate statement about teaching across the curriculum?

    a. This is a method of planning a lesson so general that it can apply to any content area
    b. Career planning for students is better addressed by other, more specific methods
    c. Application of school subjects to life is best served by different methods than this
    d. A single lesson plan includes math, English, reading, social studies, art, science, etc.

48. Which of the following is the most correct statement about manipulatives for teaching math in grades K-12?

    a. They are only efficacious when they are actual physical objects
    b. They help make an abstract subject more concrete for learners
    c. They are not yet available virtually on PC and so would not work
    d. They actively engage student's less than traditional math classes

49. Educational researchers have identified three main criteria for choosing instructional media. Which of the following is NOT one of these?

    a. Instructor facilitation
    b. Practicality of the media
    c. Student appropriateness
    d. Instructional appropriateness

50. A number of researchers identify constraints upon selection of instructional media. Which of the following choices is NOT an identified constraint that can hinder choosing media?

    a. Production factors
    b. Instructor facilitation
    c. Availability of materials
    d. Student appropriateness

51. Which of the following instructional media will meet all of a teacher's criteria for a specific lesson by showing motion, reproducing sounds, *and* allowing student interaction?

    a. Chalkboard or easel
    b. Computer software
    c. Textbook/handouts
    d. Overhead projector

52. When assessing student behavior, which data collection method gathers information about outcomes of behavior rather than the behavior itself?

    a. Behavioral checklists
    b. Behavioral interview
    c. Permanent products
    d. Observational data

53. Which of the following methods of collecting observational data of student behavior is most indicated for a behavior which seems to occur constantly?

    a. Event recording
    b. Duration recording
    c. Latency recording
    d. Interval recording

54. Which type of graph is used most often for showing a set of collected data?

    a. A bar graph
    b. A basic line graph
    c. A ratio graph
    d. A cumulative graph

55. The purpose of a functional behavior assessment is to determine…

    a. Why a behavior occurs
    b. What the behavior is
    c. When a behavior occurs
    d. How a behavior occurs

56. In conducting a functional behavior assessment of a student's problem behavior, what is an example of direct assessment?

    a. Interviewing the student who exhibits the problem behavior
    b. Interviewing the teacher of the student with the behavior
    c. Observation and recording of the behavior and conditions
    d. Giving behavioral scales, checklists, and/or questionnaires

57. When a student engages in a problem behavior, assessment can show its relation to a deficit. Which of the following is most related to student motivation?

    a. Skill deficit
    b. Performance deficit
    c. A or B
    d. None of the above

58. Positive behavioral interventions are most likely to…

    a. Control the problem behavior
    b. Suppress the problem behavior
    c. Replace the problem behavior
    d. Analyze the problem behavior

59. The ABC approach to behavior analysis stands for…

    a. Alphabetical classifying
    b. Analysis Brings Changes
    c. Appropriate Behavioral Choices
    d. Antecedent-Behavior-Consequence

60. Teachers who incorporate positive behavioral supports and interventions (PBSI) into their daily instruction find it very effective for teaching replacement behaviors. What is name of the technique they are practicing?

    a. Curricular integration
    b. Curricular modification
    c. Curricular sequencing
    d. Curricular practical training

61. In normal receptive language development, at what age do babies recognize the sound of your voice?

    a. 3-6 months
    b. 2-4 months
    c. 0-3 months
    d. Upon birth

62. Between four and six months of age, what is a typical expressive language characteristic of normally developing babies?

    a. Babbling and vocal play
    b. Differentiation of cries
    c. Smiling, cooing, and gooing
    d. Saying their first words

63. The component of language structure that involves the production and reception of speech sounds is called…

    a. Morphology
    b. Phonology
    c. Semantics
    d. Syntax

64. Misplaced modifiers, dangling participles, and lack of subject-verb agreement in a student's writing all pertain to errors of…

    a. Phonology
    b. Morphology
    c. Semantics
    d. Syntax

65. A student who has difficulty understanding spoken language has a deficit in…

    a. Expressive communication
    b. Receptive communication
    c. Verbal communication
    d. Social communication

66. Which assistive technology is most appropriate for a student with a voice disorder that interferes with audible speech production?

    a. Speech-to-text computer software
    b. Text-to-speech computer software
    c. Voice recognition computer software
    d. Voice synthesizer computer software

67. For a student with intellectual disabilities and cerebral palsy, including symptoms of spastic quadriplegia and hand contractures, which alternative communication system is most appropriate?

    a. An electronic talking book
    b. A notebook of communication symbols
    c. A communication board and adapted pointer
    d. A computer equipped with adaptive keyboard

68. In core activities to teach phonological awareness, what would typically be introduced the earliest?

    a. Phoneme blending
    b. Phoneme segmenting
    c. Phoneme identification
    d. Phoneme substitution

69. Phonemic drills are most appropriate for remediating which of the following?

    a. Voice disorders
    b. Fluency disorders
    c. Language disorders
    d. Articulation disorders

70. Which of the following is true about reading?

    a. Students can best learn to read through reading to learn
    b. Students can learn to read and read to learn concurrently
    c. Students cannot read to learn until after learning to read
    d. Students in early grades will not read unless it is to learn

71. Which of the following reading activities features shared reading?

    a. Readers' theaters
    b. Book clubs
    c. Literature circles
    d. Literature focus groups

72. What statement is true regarding literacy?

    a. The same literacy skills in students apply across subjects
    b. The literacy demands of society have changed over time
    c. Literacy required of pupils stays constant across grades
    d. Literacy is best taught in the schools in a separate lesson

73. Of the following, which is most typical of students with reading disorders?

    a. Their comprehension is poor whether reading silently or aloud
    b. They often read rapidly but with poor comprehension
    c. They read every word but do not understand all of them
    d. They do not necessarily have problems with spelling

74. Which of these is true about frequent signs of reading problems?

    a. Decoding problems with sentences/paragraphs rather than with syllables/words
    b. To recognize many vocabulary words is less of a problem than to decode words
    c. The ability to identify vocabulary words on sight in reading text is usually limited
    d. Difficulty understanding rhymes or the order of sounds is a less common issue

75. Which of the following is correct about findings related to reading disabilities in children?

    a. Children with reading disabilities usually have normal speech-language development

    b. Children with reading disabilities and those with writing problems are in separate groups

    c. Children with reading disabilities and those with math problems are in separate groups

    d. Children with reading disabilities are found to have difficulties with finger recognition

76. Of the following, which statement is accurate regarding early activities with children to promote print awareness?

    a. Upper case letters, lower case letters, and sounds should be taught in combination

    b. Using mnemonics that incorporates letters into pictures is effective for print awareness

    c. When teaching children upper and lower case letters, teach upper case letters first

    d. When teaching children, multiple sensory modes should be avoided as distractions

77. When advertising and other media use the word "LOOK!" with the two O's depicted as eyes, this association mimics which of Ehri's (1995) phases of sight word recognition?

    a. Partial alphabetic

    b. Pre-alphabetic

    c. Full alphabetic

    d. Consolidated

78. When students can recognize letter combinations, such as /str/ or /ough/, that are found in the spelling of many words as patterns, they have reached which of Ehri's (1995) phases of sight word recognition?

    a. Consolidated alphabetic

    b. Partial alphabetic

    c. Pre-alphabetic

    d. Full alphabetic

79. In which of Ehri's (1995) phases of sight word recognition do students find it easy to differentiate among similarly spelled words like "mat," "mart," and "mate"?

    a. Pre-alphabetic phase

    b. Partial alphabetic

    c. Consolidated alphabetic

    d. Full alphabetic

80. Which of the following statements is correct about recognition of letter combinations that occur across many words?

    a. This ability interferes with automaticity of word recognition

    b. This ability undermines accurate word recognition in reading

    c. This ability decreases the demand on the reader's memory

    d. This ability is a separate development from reading fluency

81. What statement is accurate regarding research findings about methods for teaching reading fluency?

    a. Assisted reading approaches have been found highly effective for fluency

    b. Repeated reading and assisted reading approaches are mutually exclusive

    c. Assisted reading methods work equally well one-on-one and in regular classrooms

    d. Reading while listening is more efficient but unrelated to assisted reading

82. Which of the following characteristics of proficient readers *most* relies on metacognition?

    a. Knowledge of correspondence between symbols and sounds
    b. An understanding of the syntactic structures in reading matter
    c. The ability to self-monitor to develop reading comprehension
    d. Being knowledgeable about semantic associations in print text

83. What is a true finding about the qualities of students who read well?

    a. They tend to focus on one central strategy for reading comprehension
    b. Hypotheses, ideas synthesis, and conclusions are parts of their reading
    c. Because they love to read, they do not need a reason for reading texts
    d. They are not slowed down by having to reread previous sections of text

84. The following teaching strategies all promote reading proficiency. Which one is more related to practice than to motivation?

    a. Providing choices in the reading materials for students
    b. Finding ways to make reading meaningful to students
    c. Finding ways to make reading fun for students
    d. Providing the students with many opportunities to read

85. Ms. Ross introduces new vocabulary words to her class daily. She then assigns reading that includes these words, uses those words in her speech as she presents lessons, and points them out when they appear in other contexts. Which instructional method does this represent?

    a. Appropriate word choice
    b. Teaching of word analysis
    c. Using contextual analysis
    d. Multiple word exposures

86. Mr. Law wants to facilitate his high school students' ability to expand their vocabulary. He seizes the opportunity when a student comes in perplexed at having seen the word "antidisestablishmentarianism." He asks the class, "What parts of this word have you seen before in other words?" One student volunteers that he recognizes "anti-" from "antibiotic;" another says "Anti-Trust Law." A third student then identifies "dis-" from "disability" and a fourth says "dislike." Most of the class then sees the next parts as "establish" or "establishment." He then asks them if they have seen other words ending in "-ary" and, following their responses, "-ism." What technique is Mr. Law using?

    a. Multiple exposures to a word
    b. Choosing appropriate words
    c. Making a contextual analysis
    d. Teaching them word analysis

87. In facilitating reading comprehension and critical thinking in students with disabilities, which of the following strategies is best for visualizing concepts?

    a. Teaching summarization
    b. Using graphic organizers
    c. Using multiple strategies
    d. Teaching story structure

88. Which of the following is NOT an example of a graphic organizer?
   a. Visual imagery
   b. Venn diagram
   c. Concept maps
   d. Flow chart

89. A teacher explicates a poet's use of symbolism and metaphor in a short poem to a high school class, showing how he uses an animal to represent an idea ("The Thought-Fox" by Ted Hughes). She is pleasantly shocked when a student who had seemed thoroughly unimpressed with her poetry unit suddenly expresses appreciation by saying, "So this is really good." When she asks him to elaborate, he responds, "It's really good because you can relate it to something that's real in your life." Which teaching strategy that enhances reading proficiency is most related to this outcome?
   a. Making reading material meaningful to the student
   b. Making the activity of reading fun for the students
   c. Making reading include choices made by a student
   d. Making ample opportunities for students to read

90. A student with disabilities does not demonstrate certain adaptive life skills such as cleaning up a work area at school, but his parents report that he has done so at home for years. An ecological assessment finds he does not demonstrate these skills in any other settings. Which instructional procedure is most appropriate for this student?
   a. Re-teaching him these skills
   b. Teaching skill generalization
   c. Teaching skill maintenance
   d. Teaching skill discrimination

91. Which of the following is true about self-determination and self-advocacy for students with disabilities?
   a. Federal legislation for disabilities does not specifically address self-determination
   b. Students with disabilities develop these skills like other students but at older ages
   c. Some special education programs for self-advocacy use student-directed curricula
   d. Student-led IEP conferences do not benefit the self-advocacy of disabled students

92. What is correct regarding skills that students with disabilities need to engage in self-determination and self-advocacy?
   a. Self-awareness supports social skills rather than self-determination
   b. Managing one's own transition plans is a minor part of self-advocacy
   c. To take part in training programs, students must be able to set goals
   d. Self-advocacy programs train for self-monitoring and self-evaluation

93. Which of the following is true about explicit self-advocacy instruction for students with learning disabilities, emotional or behavior disorders, and other high-incidence disabilities?
   a. Learning the skills taught is more important than understanding their value
   b. Opportunities to practice skills rather than to observe them are paramount
   c. In this instruction, students need to be given immediate progress feedback
   d. Skills are generalized to real settings through doing, not through instruction

94. The stage of career development wherein students can develop self-confidence and a sense of self-worth is known as...
    a. Career exploration
    b. Career orientation
    c. Career preparation
    d. Career placement

95. Introducing each of the stages of career development for students with disabilities should be determined *most* by which of the following?
    a. The student's developmental level
    b. The student's grade level in school
    c. The student's level of experience
    d. The student's chronological age

96. Which of the following is *most* accurate about exceptional students who are gifted?
    a. They typically have advanced social skills
    b. Their academic performance is superior
    c. Their IQ scores indicate their giftedness
    d. They are often found socially immature

97. During which stage of career development should students be given opportunities for a variety of occupationally related hands-on experiences?
    a. Career awareness
    b. Career exploration
    c. Career preparation
    d. Career placement

98. Representatives from outside agencies attending a high school student's IEP meeting to assist with transition planning include someone from the transportation agency and an assistive technology expert. To which domain of transition planning are these representatives most related?
    a. Personal and social
    b. Employment/career
    c. Community living
    d. Leisure/recreation

99. When does current federal legislation (IDEA 2004) require transition planning for students with disabilities to begin?
    a. At age 18
    b. At age 22
    c. At age 14
    d. At age 16

100. Of the following resources that support students with disabilities in transitions from school to work, which are designed to connect schools with community agencies/services?
    a. WorkAbility programs and/or TPPs
    b. Regional Occupational Programs
    c. State Conservation Corps
    d. The Job Corps

Answer Key and Explanations

1. B: The Education for all Handicapped Children, or Education for the Handicapped Act (EHA) was passed in 1975 (Public Law #94-142) to guarantee everyone with disabilities aged 5-21 a Free Appropriate Public Education/FAPE (C). It stated that all students with disabilities must be educated as much as possible in the Least Restrictive Environment/LRE (D). In 1990, this law was reauthorized and renamed the Individuals with Disabilities Education Act/IDEA (A). It was later amended in successive reauthorizations in 1991, 1997, and 2004.

2. D: Under the 2004 amendments to the IDEA, procedural safeguards state that a due process hearing can be requested not only by the child's parents (A), not only by the parents or school (B), and not only by the parents' attorney (C), but by the parents, the school/public agency, or their attorneys.

3. C: The Family Education Rights and Privacy Act (FERPA) and the Privacy Rule for student health records of the Health Insurance Portability and Accountability Act (HIPAA) are founded on the same basic legal and ethical principles. FERPA is designed to protect confidential information in students' school records pertaining to education, and HIPAA is designed to protect any confidential health information that is individually identifiable, including student health records in public schools or in any schools covered by FERPA.

4. B. After a student is identified via "Child Find" or referred to special education services by a teacher, parent, social services, or others, assessments are conducted to evaluate whether or not the student has a disability and, if so, to diagnose the specific disability and establish performance baselines for planning interventions and for comparison in evaluating progress. After this, professionals and the student's parent(s) together assess whether the student is eligible as defined by IDEA. If the child is determined to be eligible, the IEP team will then gather to discuss and write the student's IEP.

5. B: The pre-referral stage of the IEP process includes interventions and other activities in the general education classroom to screen students before any formal referral is made for special education. Testing classroom accommodations and modifications for effectiveness is one of these activities. If accommodations, validated teaching methods, instructional modifications, consultation and help from specialists do not remedy learning problems, the next step is referral. After that, identification (A) is made and eligibility (C) is determined for special education services. Review (D) of the IEP is made after it has been implemented to evaluate progress and, if necessary, change the IEP.

6. D: None of choices provided would determine a child as having a disability. IDEA's special rule (Section 300.306, Determination of Eligibility) states that a child must not be determined as having a disability due to lack of appropriate instruction in reading (A) or in math (B), or due to a lack of proficiency with the English language (C).

7. A: The 2004 amendments to the law prohibit requiring a severe discrepancy between intellectual ability, competence, school achievement, or performance to identify specific learning disabilities (SLD). Prior to this amendment, many educators looked for such a discrepancy as a sign of SLDs. The law does not require finding such a discrepancy (B), nor does it require ability and achievement to be similar (C). IDEA's 2004 reauthorization does directly address the issue of comparing competence and performance (D).

8. C: The effects of spina bifida vary in severity with the type of spina bifida and the individual who has it, but the most likely effect is on motor development as the spinal column does not fuse completely, leaving an opening. Many children with spina bifida cannot walk, and the strength and mobility of the upper limbs and body can also be affected. Intellectual development (A) can be affected if cerebrospinal fluid backs up into the brain and the fluid buildup, called hydrocephalus, is not relieved by shunting; spina bifida without hydrocephalus does not cause brain damage. As long as intellectual development is not affected, language development (B) is not affected by spina bifida. This condition per se does not affect social development (D) as, for example, autism often does.

9. D: Children with autism spectrum disorders often have deficits in social skills, communication skills, and joint or shared attention. They tend to prefer focusing individual attention on one activity or subject for sustained periods and may have difficulty with transitions. Children with attention deficit disorder (C) have difficulty focusing and sustaining their attention, are easily distracted, have short attention spans and tend to jump from one thing to another. Children with intellectual disabilities secondary to Down syndrome (A) and those with overall developmental delays (B) are likely to have shorter attention spans and less ability to focus.

10. B: Children with congenital rubella, or who are exposed in utero to maternal rubella, are NOT more likely to suffer paralysis. Rubella (German measles) causes birth defects related to the sensory systems of vision and hearing. Babies exposed to rubella are more likely to suffer from deafness (A), blindness (C), and/or cataracts (D) of the eyes, which interfere with normal vision.

11. C: By law, in most states a major review of the IEP is required every year (A), but in some states it is required every three years (B) according to an IDEA 2004 pilot study to save on paperwork and administrative duties (as of 2007, 15 states were participating), so IEPs are reviewed either annually or triennially by state. Beyond these two intervals, reviews do not vary in frequency by each state (D).

12. A: Executive function includes planning, organizing, keeping track of time, keeping track of multiple things, relating earlier learning to current learning, and other higher cognitive activities. Self-regulation (B) relates only to talking out of turn in class, and is just one component of executive function. Sequencing (C) involves arranging items in the correct order (chronological, logical, etc.), and is also one specific aspect of executive function. Memory (D), or retaining and retrieving information, requires using mental strategies that are included in executive function.

13. A: Whichever professional is best able to explain what the student's test results imply for the student's education should interpret those results for the IEP team members. Which professional varies: it could be the student's special education teacher, who will be an IEP team member (A); it could be the school psychologist, who may or may not be on the student's IEP team (C); or it could be another professional who is not on the IEP team (D), because being a member of the IEP team is not required for this function. The important factor is the ability to relate assessment results to educational planning and programming that will address needs and strengths identified in those results.

14. B: The COACH model (Giangreco, Cloninger and Iverson, 1998) is a collaborative approach described by educational researchers as "student-directed planning," which they claim goes "beyond person-centered planning" (Wehmeyer et al, 2002) by making the student central in the process. Person-centered planning typically centers more on family and social support systems. GAP (Turnbull & Turnbull, 2002) (A); MAPs (Pearpoint, Forest, & O'Brien, 1996) (C); and PATH (D), which extends the MAPs process to develop "a more definitive plan of action," are all examples of person-centered planning.

15. D: The National Council on Disability is an independent federal agency that makes recommendations to the President and Congress regarding issues related to disabilities. The FCSN (A) is an organization founded in Boston, Massachusetts that informs, helps, and supports parents of children with disabilities, involved professionals, and communities. The CPAS (B), formed by the University of California, San Francisco (UCSF) through a grant from the National Institute on Disability and Rehabilitation Research (NIDRR), supplies research, dissemination, training, and technical help with personal assistance services concerns nationwide. The NRDN (C) represents the needs of its members in Protection and Advocacy (P&A) before federal agencies and Congress, but is not itself a federal agency and does not make recommendations to the president.

16. C: The primary purpose of universal newborn hearing screenings is early identification of hearing loss, which affords early intervention. Professional organizations such as ASHA advocate universal screening because not all infants are screened even though hearing loss is the most common congenital disability. Educational planning (A) is a purpose of later educational testing of a child, not of newborn hearing screening. Disability diagnosis (B) requires a complete audiological evaluation defining type, degree, and configuration of hearing loss instead of just a screening, because that only identifies presence or absence of hearing loss. Eligibility for special education services under the IDEA (D) is a purpose of later, comprehensive assessments of preschool- and school-aged students, not infants.

17. D: Summative assessments are given after instruction, such as tests at the ends of chapters, units, semesters, or terms; school district interim assessments or benchmark assessments; standardized state tests, etc. As such, they are often used to evaluate the effectiveness of instruction. Authentic assessments (A) are made in real-life situations, such as driver's license tests, or in simulations of real life. Ongoing assessments (B) are like formative assessments (C) in that they are made during instruction rather than after it. Formative assessments can be equated with practice that students receive as part of instruction, rather than scoring or grading what has already been learned as summative assessments do.

18. C: The 2004 IDEA reauthorization does not provide for avoiding different test languages. It provides that local educational agencies ensure that assessments "are provided and administered in the language... most likely to yield accurate information on what the child knows and can do academically, developmentally, and functionally." This was amended from the previous wording, "provided and administered in the child's native language or other mode of communication." IDEA 2004 also provides that a variety of instruments and methods be used (A) instead of only one, that assessment results are used to determine disability (B), and that the impacts of cognitive and behavioral factors be assessed as well as physical and developmental ones (D).

19. B: It is congruent with general ethical principles maintained by most professional organizations that, when there is clear and present danger to an individual or to society, an assessor should break confidentiality regarding assessment results. Ethical principles dictate that assessors should not informally disclose student test results to other school employees (A). It is also considered unethical to report students' assessment results formally before obtaining their parents' consent (C) if they are minors (or the student's consent if the student is not a minor). Ethical principles additionally require that an assessor avoid assessing culturally diverse students if that assessor does not demonstrate the cultural competence to do so because assessing them regardless (D) would be inappropriate.

20. A: Norm-referenced tests compare the student's score to norms, such as national averages of scores for students of the same age or grade level. These are standardized tests, such as national achievement tests including the SAT, ACT, GRE, etc. Criterion-referenced tests (B) do not compare students' scores to other students' scores, but rather measure students' performance against a criterion, standard, or objective previously determined and given to students before testing. Class quizzes, exams, oral reports, presentations, experiments, and performance-based tests (C) are examples of criterion-referenced tests. Ipsative measures or tests (D) compare the student's performance to his/her own previous performance.

21. C: Criterion-referenced tests encourage cooperation because they do not compare students and are oriented toward mastery, meaning that every student is expected to succeed. They do not tend to promote competition (A). Norm-referenced tests are not good for assessing instructional effectiveness (B) because they cover wide ranges in their content and are standardized, so local/state instructional content often differs from that in the tests. For the same reasons, norm-referenced tests are also not useful for making individual student diagnoses (D).

22. A: Jim's instruction can be considered quite effective, as he has not only scored 90 percent on classroom performance assessments and met or surpassed his IEP goals, but he has also increased his score on national norm-referenced standardized tests by 15 percent in a year. Scoring 20 percent below national norms does not indicate that his instruction is not effective enough (B) because (1) norm-referenced tests are not useful for determining instructional effectiveness, as state and local teaching practices vary too much for the broad range of content on these tests to apply; and (2) because Jim has mild cognitive impairment and may or may not ever score equally with national averages. Because norm-referenced tests do not indicate instructional effectiveness, working on his instruction just to raise his scores on these tests (C) is unnecessary. More information is not needed (D) to know that he is demonstrating progress, so his instructional program must be working.

23. B: Norm-referenced tests compare individual student scores to national averages. With the majority of school populations taking these standardized tests, plotting their scores will yield a normal distribution, or "bell curve," where the majority had average scores and minorities had higher- and lower-than-average scores. Criterion-referenced measures (A) measure individual students' results against a criterion previously established by the teacher, school, or district but do not compare them, so there would be no distribution. As criterion-referenced measures, performance-based assessments (C) would also not show a distribution. Portfolio assessments (D) are made by teachers of individual students' portfolios of work produced over time. These typically are not meant to be compared with other students' work, so there is no statistical distribution.

24. D: In analytical scoring, the teacher makes a detailed evaluation and uses a rubric or a scale to attribute points to varying performance levels, thus yielding several scores. A narrative evaluation (A) typically does not give scores at all, but describes the child's attainments, skills, or knowledge and strengths and needs. General impression scoring (B) uses a scale, such as 1-10, which yields a single score. Focused holistic scoring (C) is brief and not in-depth, and works by seeking some factor or attribute identified earlier, and yields only one score.

25. C: Any kind of observational assessment will involve direct observation of Keith's behavior, which is what the teacher wants to evaluate. If the teacher uses the same recording methods as for behavioral baseline measures, comparing current results to baseline can indicate Keith's progress. Norm-referenced tests (A) are standardized tests and typically measure academic achievement, not behavior. Interviewing Keith (B) is contraindicated because he has expressive language deficits and may have difficulty responding, and also because observing what the student does is more accurate than asking the student to describe his own behavior. Curriculum-based testing (D) connects assessment to instruction. While behavioral interventions have probably been incorporated during

Keith's classroom instruction, curriculum-based assessments are related to curriculum content areas, not behavioral issues.

26. D: According to the 29th Annual Report to Congress on the Implementation of the Individuals with Disabilities Education Act (IDEA) made in 2007, data for 2005 show that African-American and Native American (including Alaskan) students were respectively 1.54 and 1.47 times as likely (the two groups averaged 1.505) to receive special education services under the IDEA as all other students. Therefore, they were far less than 3.2 times (C) as likely and less than twice (B) as likely to receive these services, but much more than half (A) as likely to receive them as students from all other racial/ethnic groups combined.

27. A: The 2007 29th Annual Report to Congress on the Implementation of the IDEA found that, in 2005, 45.5 percent of students aged 6-21 who received special education services under this law were diagnosed with specific learning disabilities. 18.9 percent had speech-language impairments. 9.2 percent had other health impairments. 8.9 percent were diagnosed with intellectual disabilities, and 7.7 percent had diagnoses of emotional disturbance.

28. B: Like most tests, the standardized test was designed by white people and oriented to upper-middle-class white culture. Unlike the white people who designed the tests, the students in this scenario come from families that did not own dishware with matching cups and saucers. Their association was logical as they placed a cup directly on a table. This demonstrates a cultural bias in assessment that may be overlooked. Only a few IQ tests are "culture-fair" (e.g., Cattell), and even fewer are written exclusively by and for African-American culture (e.g., Black Intelligence Test of Cultural Homogeneity/"BITCH-100 Test" [Williams, 1972]; Dove Counterbalance General Intelligence Test/"Chitling Test" 1971). While some children of impoverished families are deprived of cultural/intellectual stimulation at home (A), some are not. Regardless, this did not cause the so-called "error." While teachers from predominant cultures may have biases, the choice was not from lack of instruction (C), but different home experiences. Though colloquial language differs among American subcultures, this instance did not involve lack of comprehension (D).

29. A: A student's ability to retell a story s/he has heard assesses the degree of auditory comprehension. An informal reading inventory (B) can assess a student's reading fluency, reading comprehension, etc., rather than assessing the student's understanding of what s/he hears. Curriculum-based assessment (C) tests whether students have learned the curriculum content taught through a broad approach, rather than focusing testing on a specific learning skill area like auditory comprehension, which is not a content area. Periodic fluency checking (D) is a way to monitor students' reading fluency rather than their listening comprehension.

30. C: In scientifically based research, validity means that something measures what it claims to measure. Being able to repeat measurements with consistent results (A) refers to reliability, not validity. Validity does not refer to a general consensus of opinion (B). Subjective opinions should not influence conclusions in scientific research because conclusions should be based on objective data. While addressing significant questions (D) is a feature of scientific research, it is not a definition of validity.

31. B: In scientifically based research, reliability means that a test or measurement can be repeated and consistently yield comparable results each time. Measuring or testing what it is meant to measure or test (A) is a definition of validity, not reliability. Reliability does not mean trustworthiness based on a lot of previous research (C) or that a measure is proven by having been used for many years (D); it simply means that if it is repeated, it will yield similar results with every repetition.

32. D: In scientifically based research, the researchers must always have other possible explanations for any conclusions they draw from their studies. They must also seek any evidence to contradict what they conclude. The main features of scientific research are the same across all fields of study and do not differ (A). Scientific research is not used to address any questions individual researchers find most interesting (B), but is aimed at addressing relatively significant questions like those involved in core issues within the field. For example, in special education, a significant question for research might be "What are the most effective strategies for teaching students with learning disabilities how to read?" Reputable journals do make peer review a prerequisite for publication (C), and rigorous peer review is one of the features of scientific research.

33. A: Generalization of learning is the ability to apply learning across multiple and varied contexts or settings. Regular practice and periodic testing (B) are designed to promote maintenance rather than generalization. Learning one step at a time (C) is a characteristic of task analysis, which breaks complex skills or tasks down into more achievable steps and is related to promoting skill acquisition rather than generalization. Practicing a new skill before applying it to real-life situations (D) is a way to promote both acquisition and maintenance of the skill before its application and generalization.

34. B: A student's IEP team does determine his/her eligibility for an alternate curriculum program. These programs are not the first choice for students with disabilities (A) and are not preferred over general curricula with accommodations and/or modifications (C). Rather, if an individual student still finds the general education curriculum too demanding even with accommodations and modifications provided, then an alternate curriculum program is a placement to consider. Students typically are not still assigned to general education classrooms in these programs (D); usually they are assigned to a special education classroom, but have general education classes and enrichment activities throughout their school day where they can interact with students without disabilities.

35. C: Special education teachers specialize in both assessment and adaptations. They should be familiar with a variety of assessment instruments; know which ones to select for an individual student, how to administer them, and how to interpret their results relative to specific disabilities; and be able to identify particular disabilities based on assessment results. They should also have expertise in making adaptations in testing, curricula, and materials that enable students with disabilities to access the general education curriculum as much as possible, and/or allow them to obtain a free, appropriate public education.

36. D: In Lev Vygotsky's social-cognitive theory, the concept of scaffolding refers to support that is provided to learners (by parents, teachers, other adults, peers, etc.) when they need it to learn a task or skill, and which is gradually withdrawn as the learner becomes more able to perform that task or skill independently. It is a form of support for all learners, not just special needs children, and it is not always there (B), but is decreased little by little corresponding to the learner's progress. It is not a structural framework for a lesson (A) or for social interactions (C).

37. C: Bandura's social learning theory incorporates observational learning, vicarious learning, and imitation of modeling. He found through his research that a child could observe another child receiving a reward or punishment and learn the same things through observation that the other child learned through direct experience. The belief that hands-on learning (A) was superior to observation was supported by Jean Piaget, not Bandura. Rather famously, Bandura also discovered that children who viewed violent videos did display more aggressive behavior as a result; observation of real-life aggression was not required (B). Bandura's pioneering work made parents and educators more aware of the impacts that media can have on children's behavior (D).

38. B: It is important for teachers to include needed classroom adaptations in their comprehensive plans for students with disabilities. Many of the classroom changes that teachers make are incidental but provide an immediate solution when they notice some students having difficulties; this is not rare (A). These kinds of changes are usually both necessary and appropriate, not the reverse (C). Therefore, they are likely to meet those students' needs, not unlikely (D). However, incidental modifications alone are insufficient because as teachers come to know individual students, they should plan adaptations for the needs they can predict before starting a lesson.

39. A: One general problem that elementary school teachers face when teaching culturally diverse students is that most textbooks introduce a large number of new concepts to be taught within a short time frame. Another problem is that many of these texts' teacher editions do not offer tips for meeting the needs of culturally diverse students (B). An additional problem is that the reading levels of most texts are too difficult for many diverse students (C). As a result, teachers must differentiate their instruction for diverse students in general education classrooms because the books they use will not preclude this need (D).

40. D: Carefully planning what the content of the math instruction covers and the order in which it is taught (A), using their best judgment in choosing and applying appropriate teaching strategies (B), and designing practice activities with special needs students in mind (C) are all actions by teachers that will improve the involvement and progress of all students, including those with special needs. The action most likely to be needed specifically by some special needs students in the general education classroom is using more intensive direct instruction methods to teach them basic mathematics.

41. C: The TeacherVision authors emphasize that *"All students should have access to all information. In no way should the Planning Pyramid be thought of as a way to track students (B)... or limit expectations"* (A). This tool does not dictate a sequence in which all students will learn (D). Rather, the premise is that all students are capable of learning, but they will not necessarily learn at equal rates. The authors state that some students, for example, may move directly to the top of the pyramid depending on their prior knowledge and interest, including special needs students when supplied with the necessary adaptations.

42. B: Using multilevel teaching practices is an effective method to teach word recognition to a class of students with many reading levels and diverse needs. Giving direct instruction to individual students (A) is very effective but not efficient, and can be impossible for one teacher with typical class sizes. Creating smaller groups for each level (D) is similarly inefficient as the teacher could end up with too many groups to teach in the time allowed. Teaching to the median (C) leaves out too many students who are below or above the medium range that the median targets. Multilevel practices address a variety of reading levels and allow adaptations for special student needs.

43. D: Multilevel instructional practices can be used in various grouping arrangements, including whole class (A), small group (B), and paired (C) contexts; no one of these is better than the others. When arrangements other than whole class instruction are used, the smaller groups of students are typically still mixed in character rather than being homogeneous. Multilevel instruction is based on the principle that all students have a chance to access suitable instruction and to get support from their teachers and classmates.

44. A: Teachers will not always know a student's preferred communication mode. For example, deaf students often use sign language rather than speech. This is also true of learning modalities, such as blind students reading in Braille. Many teachers do not know either of these systems, but must be able to provide adaptations to meet these students' special needs. They can procure Braille texts without learning Braille, and they can obtain live, online, or video sign language interpreters without learning sign language. Teachers may also need to differentiate instruction based on gender because learning is not always the same for boys as it is for girls (B). Teachers are likely, especially with disability and diversity populations, to encounter age differences in one class (C). Learning English is not the sole responsibility of students (D) because many ESL/ELL programs and methods are available to teachers.

45. C: In planning lessons, teachers need to consider the skill or concept they want to teach and be sure to define it and not assume they already know what it is (A). They need to identify the prerequisites that students need to learn the new material, not assume that they already have them (B). They need to consider what is required for the students to master the material being taught (C). They should also think about how they can expand what they have taught and how to show students to apply their new learning in useful ways. Such planning is not premature (D) and should be part of the lesson plans.

46. A: Textbooks incorporate informational structure, such as presenting items in chronological order, comparisons and contrasts, and pointing out causal relationships. They also use informational features such as boldface type, sub-headings, bullet points, review questions, glossaries, an index, etc., to assist students in organizing, remembering, and applying information, even though many students may not use them. The simplest, most direct and efficient way that Mr. Stewart can help his students is to point these out and explain how to use them. Creating separate handouts (B) takes more time and work and may duplicate what the text already does. Graphic organizers (C) are excellent aids, especially for students who learn more visually than verbally, but they also involve more work than using the text. Mr. Stewart's students have good reading comprehension but cannot organize whole chapters. A Power Point® is an excellent supplement to the text, but should not replace explaining the text's informational aids.

47. D: In teaching across the curriculum, one lesson plan actually incorporates all subjects taught rather than being so generic as to apply to any subject (A). For example, a spreadsheet that uses visually beautiful graphic design incorporates math and art. Teaching across the curriculum does facilitate career planning (B) because it shows students different ways that subjects learned in school apply to real life (C), including job choices.

48. B: Manipulatives make the abstract concepts of mathematics more concrete for students, making them good choices for students whose levels of cognitive development allow more concrete than abstract thought. Historically they have been physical objects, but, this is no longer necessary with computer technology (A). Virtual manipulatives are available and are also found effective (C). For example, the University of Utah has developed (and continues to develop) the National Library of Virtual Manipulatives through a grant from the National Science Foundation. While they cannot handle virtual manipulatives like physical ones, students can still see and manipulate objects onscreen to see concept relationships and applications more concretely. These virtual programs are interactive and promote students' active engagement more than traditional math lessons typically do (D).

49. A: Instructor facilitation is identified as a constraint on using instructional media (Dick, Carey, & Carey, 2001; Strauss and Frost, 1999; and Reiser and Dick, 1996), not a selection criterion. Researchers (Reiser and Dick, 1996) identify practicality (B) as a criterion: The media should be available, understandable to the teacher, and efficient in terms of time and cost. Student appropriateness (C) is another criterion: Media chosen should be applicable to the targeted students' levels of development and experience. The third criterion is instructional appropriateness (D): The media should work with the teaching strategy planned; should afford efficient, effective lesson presentation; and should promote the students' attainment of the lesson's learning objectives.

50. D: Student appropriateness is not a constraint on choosing media but a criterion for choosing the most applicable media for the students' cognitive and developmental levels and current knowledge and experience. Production factors (A) are constraints when some media are too costly in both price and time. Instructor facilitation (B) is a constraint if the activities required of the teacher to facilitate use of certain media are excessive or overly difficult. If no materials are available (C), then the teacher has to create them, resulting in a production constraint (A).

51. B: Computer software meets all of the listed criteria. A chalkboard or easel (A) allows student interaction but does not meet the other requirements. Textbooks and handouts (C) do not fulfill any of the criteria, though they have many other desirable characteristics (portability, allowing highlighting/writing/drawing in or on them, availability after the lesson, independent use, etc.). Overhead projector (D) presentations (and Power Point® or other computer presentations) allow writing/highlighting/drawing, let students control the pace, are easily modified, etc., but they do not meet these other specific criteria either.

52. C: Permanent products reflect the outcomes of certain behaviors. Examples are worksheets, tests of mastery of a subject or skill, or environmental outcomes, such as a work area that the student has cleaned up. The following all gather information about behaviors per se rather than their outcomes. Behavioral checklists (A) are completed by parents, teachers, or others familiar with a student and the student's behavior. Behavioral interviews (B) are conducted with adults or children about a student's behavior. Observational data (D) are collected by someone who observes the student and records the target behavior on a data sheet when it occurs.

53. D: Interval recording is best for a behavior which seems constant or nearly so. By marking whether a behavior occurs during specified short time intervals (e.g., 10 seconds, 30 seconds, one minute, or two minutes) on a data sheet, the observer can provide an estimate of how many times a high-frequency behavior occurs. Event recording (A) is better suited for less frequent behaviors of shorter duration. The observer counts the number of times the behavior occurs during a specified period, such as a 30-minute lesson. Duration recording (B) is best for determining how long a behavior continues (for example, out-of-seat behavior) using a stopwatch or clock. Latency recording (C) can be used for measuring how long a student takes to respond to teacher instructions.

54. B: A basic line graph is the most commonly used for data. Points corresponding to numbers are plotted along the horizontal/X axis, corresponding to times or periods along the vertical/Y axis, connected by lines. Bar graphs (A) represent data similarly to line graphs, but instead of points, solid bars extend from 0 to the number indicated. Ratio graphs (C) show intervals between values according to their ratio to one another. The distance between 1 and 2 is the same as between 2 and 3 on a linear graph, but on a ratio graph, the distance between 1 and 2 is the same as between 3 and 6 because each has a ratio of 1:2. This makes relationships and comparisons visual, and is useful for showing changes in two things on one graph. Cumulative graphs (D) show running totals over time, visualizing greater or lesser ongoing growth rather than comparisons between individual values.

55. A: The purpose of a functional behavior assessment (FBA) is to determine the behavior's function, or why it occurs. This is based on the rationale that all behaviors are emitted for a reason. What the behavior is (B), or a definition of the behavior, is the first piece of the FBA. When the behavior occurs (C) is another piece of the FBA, and aids in determining the behavior's purpose, along with where it occurs, with whom, and under what conditions. How the behavior occurs (D) is a description of the behavior, which is needed for a concrete definition of the behavior.

56. C: When someone (usually an IEP team member) observes and records the student's problem behavior as well as the conditions under which it occurs, such as what happens before and after the behavior and when, where, and with whom it occurs, etc., this is an example of direct assessment. Interviewing others about the student's behavior (B) and interviewing the student himself/herself (A) are both examples of indirect assessments, as is having teachers, parents, and others complete behavior rating scales, behavior checklists, and/or questionnaires about the behavior (D).

57. B: A student with a performance deficit has the skill or competence needed to perform certain activities, but does not do so. For example, the maladaptive behavior is more reinforcing to the student than the more adaptive one, and/or the adaptive behavior has no value for the student. This is most related to motivation. A student having a skill deficit (A) is unable to perform the adaptive behavior desired due to lacking the skill or competence to do it before lacking the motivation to do it.

58. C: Positive behavioral interventions are more effective by teaching a more appropriate behavior to replace the problem behavior. Because all behaviors have some function, a problem behavior cannot simply be eliminated; some other behavior will arise to fulfill the same purpose. Interventions to control problem behaviors (A) or to suppress them (B) are not considered positive. These tend not to be maintained over time or generalized to other situations as there is no positive replacement for the undesirable behavior. It is not the interventions that analyze the behavior (D), but the prior analysis on which the subsequent intervention is based.

59. D: Antecedents are events that occur right before a problem behavior and can trigger the behavior. Consequences are events that occur right after a problem behavior and can reinforce the behavior. The ABC model of behavior analysis examines the sequence of an antecedent occurring, which then triggers the behavior, which is then reinforced by the consequence following the behavior. Knowing what precipitates the behavior, and what rewards it, helps to determine the behavior's function, or what it accomplishes for the individual.

60. A: Based on the principle that learning taught in its context of use is superior, curricular integration is practicing the technique of integrating positive behavioral interventions into daily academic instruction. Curricular modification (B) may be used as a technique for developing positive behavioral supports or interventions, and/or for enabling students with disabilities to gain access to the general curriculum, but is not the definition of integrating PBSIs into and across the curriculum. Curricular sequencing (C) refers to teaching skills in the right order, such as following the steps in a task analysis or teaching fundamentals and/or prerequisites first. Curricular practical training (D) refers to a student's employment to satisfy an internship requirement or elective that is an integral part of the school's curriculum.

61. C: Babies will respond to the sound of any voice upon birth (D) and show recognition of a familiar voice between birth and 3 months of age by smiling or stopping their crying when they hear it. Normally developing babies will do this before they are 4 (B) or 6 (A) months old.

62. A: A baby's cries differentiate (B) to indicate different needs such as hunger, pain, etc., between birth and 3 months of age. At this age they also smile when they see their parents and make cooing and gooing sounds (C). Babies engage in vocal play and babbling (A) between 4 and 6 months of age. At this age they also use vocalizations and gestures to communicate needs and wants to parents. Babies typically start to utter their first words around the ages between 7 and 12 months.

63. B: Phonology refers to the way we produce and receive speech sounds. Morphology (A) refers to the grammatical structures of and within words. Semantics (C) refers to the meanings of words. Syntax (D) refers to word order and sentence structure.

64. D: These are all examples of syntactic errors, or errors in sentence structure. An example of a misplaced modifier is "Students in public schools with disabilities…" This sounds as if the public schools have the disabilities rather than the students. The following is an example of a dangling participle: "While growing up, my parents always told me…" This sounds as if the event being described happened while the parents were growing up instead of the child. An example of lack of subject-verb agreement is "Only a pencil and paper is needed," where the "is" should be "are." Errors of phonology (A) involve misarticulation/mispronunciation of speech sounds, like lisping or substituting /w/ for /r/. Errors of morphology (B) can be in word-building, such as "unvisible" for "invisible"; or in inflections indicating grammatical form, like saying "taked" instead of "took." Errors of semantics (C) involve incorrect meanings.

65. B: A deficit in receptive communication is reflected by difficulty understanding the spoken language that one hears. Deficits in expressive communication (A) are reflected in difficulties with speaking and may be related to language processing, as in difficulty retrieving words or constructing sentences; or to speech, as in poor articulation, stuttering, or voice problems. Verbal communication (C) refers to using words vs. nonverbal communication such as gestures, body language, and facial expression, but this term does not differentiate between expressive and receptive communication. Social communication (D) is communication used in social interactions, but understanding spoken language is not limited to social interactions (it also occurs in classes, lectures, audio/video recordings, etc.).

66. D: Computer software with a voice synthesizer produces a digital voice for those who cannot speak. Speech-to-text software (A) allows a person to speak into a computer microphone and the program produces typed text of the spoken language. This helps those who can speak but cannot write or type. Text-to-speech software (B) also produces a synthesized voice to read text, but these programs typically scan the text and read it aloud to assist those with visual impairments and reading difficulties, not to supply a substitute speaking voice. Voice recognition software (C) also transcribes spoken language into typed text, similar to the closed-captioning feature on televisions.

67. C: A communication board can have pictures as well as word labels. If the student with intellectual disabilities is not literate, the pictures will facilitate choosing symbols to communicate, and the adapted pointer can be secured into the student's contracted hand to point to pictures. A talking book (A) is more appropriate for a student with visual impairment or learning disabilities in reading. A notebook of communication symbols (B) is more appropriate for a student who can point to them without equipment or turn pages and otherwise manipulate the book, but is less useful for a student with limb paralysis and contractures. A computer with an adaptive keyboard (D) is more appropriate for a student with the literacy and ability to type. The student described could not type even on an adaptive keyboard.

68. A: Phoneme blending is taking individual phonemes and combining them into a word, like blending /s/, /u/, and /n/ to make "sun." This core activity is typically taught before phoneme segmenting (B), which is the reverse of blending, or being able to identify the individual phonemes in a given word. In this case, given the word "sun," the student can break it down into /s/, /u/, and /n/. Students are also taught segmentation of initial, middle, and final phonemes. Phoneme identification (C) follows, wherein students must identify whether a given phoneme is at the beginning, middle, or end of a given word. Phoneme substitution (D) involves the student's substituting one phoneme of a word to make another word. For example, with initial phonemes, given "cat," the student can make "sat," "mat," "hat," "bat," etc.

69. D: Articulation disorders involve distortion, omission, and/or substitution of speech sounds. Phonemic drills give students practice in producing sounds correctly. Voice disorders (A) are (outside of surgery) remediated by such therapeutic techniques as breathing support and audio feedback, among others, but not phonemic drills. Fluency disorders (B) such as stuttering are treated with a variety of techniques, including the Schwartz passive inhalation method, the Van Riper Program, Mark Power's method, Hollin's Precision Fluency Shaping, and many others, but phonemic drilling has no relation to fluency. Language disorders (C) involve difficulties with processing the language one hears, reads, speaks, and/or writes, and are remediated using many different strategies, although none of them include phonemic drilling.

70. C: Students typically learn to read through third grade and transition to reading to learn and reading for pleasure around fourth grade. While they are learning the basics, all of their attention is focused on decoding, word recognition, vocabulary, comprehension, etc., so they cannot yet move beyond these tasks to focus on subject content. Therefore they cannot best learn to read through reading to learn (A) and they cannot do both things at the same time (B). In the early grades, students are learning reading itself and will only read for this reason, rather than only reading to learn (D).

71. A: Readers' Theaters feature Shared Reading as students each play a role and they take turns reading aloud. Book clubs (B), literature circles (C), and literature focus groups (D) are all reading activities that feature guided reading rather than shared reading.

72. B: Modern society demands greater literacy today than in the past. For example, as cited by Dr. Rebecca C. Faulkner, the Air Force manual for repairing fighter planes was seven pages long in World War II and 7,000 pages long in 2008. The same literacy skills in students do not apply across all subjects (A) because different literacy skills are needed for different content areas. Literacy required of school pupils also does not stay constant across grades (C) because literacy requirements advance along with each advance in grade level. Finally, literacy is not best taught in schools as a separate lesson (D) because that would be insufficient; in order to meet the changing demands of society, literacy must be taught and incorporated throughout the school day.

73. A: Students with reading disorders typically have poor reading comprehension whether they are reading silently or aloud. They do not typically read rapidly (B); a common characteristic of reading disorders is slow reading speeds, both silently and aloud. They do not typically read every word (C); students with reading disorders commonly omit or overlook some words as they read. In actuality, nearly all students with reading disorders are also found to have problems with spelling (D).

74. C: Students with reading problems frequently have trouble recognizing very many vocabulary words on sight in reading text. They also often have problems decoding (sounding out) syllables and single words (A). Sight word vocabulary and word decoding are both common difficulties; one is not less of a problem than the other (B). Another common issue is trouble understanding rhyming words and/or phonemic sequencing (D).

75. D: Children with reading disabilities are found (Fletcher et al) to have difficulty with differentiating among fingers. This was found to have implications for writing because fine motor skill indices such as finger tapping, finger succession, repetition, and localization were all found to relate to writing (Rutberg and Berninger). Children with reading disabilities are found more likely than those without reading disabilities to experience delays in their spoken language (A), to have difficulties with writing (B), and to have mathematics disabilities as well (C).

76. B: Educational experts recommend using mnemonics with letters incorporated in pictures as an effective print awareness activity. For example, the letter "f" can be drawn with stems and leaves to look like a flower, an object whose identifying word begins with "f." Associating the picture with the word and its initial letter reinforces the verbal concepts via visual imagery, making them less abstract and combining modalities. Educators advise teaching upper case letters, lower case letters, and sounds separately rather than together (A). They also recommend teaching the lower case letters first, not the upper case (C). They additionally find using multisensory modalities to be helpful, not distracting (D). For example, finger paints or letters made of sandpaper engage the tactile sense and associate it with print for young children.

77. B: In Ehri's pre-alphabetic phase of sight word recognition, children recognize words by associating their visual appearance with their meaning, as in the "LOOK" example, or with their sound. The association is not between letters and sounds and is thus termed pre-alphabetic. This phase is in the earliest stage of reading. The successive partial alphabetic (A), full alphabetic (C) and consolidated (D) alphabetic phases occur later and all involve letter-sound associations, albeit incomplete in the partial alphabetic phase.

78. A: The consolidated alphabetic phase moves beyond full alphabetic (D) coding in that the student can identify recurring patterns of combined letters in the spelling system (e.g., /str/ in "astronomy," "strong," "instruct," "strap," etc.) in addition to recognizing different words. In the pre-alphabetic (C) phase, associations between orthography and phonemics are not yet developed. In the partial alphabetic (B) phase, these associations are developed, but not as completely as they will become in the full alphabetic phase.

79. D: Students can tell similarly spelled words apart in the full alphabetic phase because, in this phase, they are now familiar enough with how most conventional spellings represent speech sounds, which helps them to pronounce new words by their spelling. In this phase, students can also immediately recognize familiar words, including those with irregular spellings that cannot be decoded. The correlation of symbols to sounds for decoding is not a feature of the pre-alphabetic phase (A). This ability has begun to develop in the partial alphabetic (B) phase. In addition to distinguishing among similarly spelled words and immediately recognizing frequently seen words, students can recognize patterns of letter combinations across the vocabulary in the consolidated alphabetic (C) phase.

80. C: The ability to identify letter combinations found in the spelling of many words, which emerges in the consolidated alphabetic phase of sight word recognition (Ehri, 1995), lessens the demand on the reader's memory because they recognize them as units, not single letters, and as common patterns within the orthographic system. As a result, this ability also promotes automaticity (A) and accuracy (B) of word recognition, which are essential parts of reading fluency (D).

81. A: A number of researchers have found that assisted reading methods achieve significant improvements in students' reading fluency. Methods using repeated readings can be both unassisted and assisted (B). Assisted reading methods, because of the need for one-on-one instruction, have been found more workable in tutoring, but too time-intensive to be incorporated successfully in traditional classrooms (C). Reading while listening takes less time by being adapted using recordings for instruction of a group rather than individual students. It is thus more efficient than assisted reading, but it is not unrelated (D) because it was adapted from assisted reading.

82. C: Metacognition is the knowledge and regulation of one's own cognitive processes, and is often described as "thinking about thinking." Proficient readers most rely on metacognition to engage in self-monitoring while they read, thus promoting comprehension. Knowing how spelling and speech sounds correspond with one another (A), understanding word order and sentence structure in reading material (B), and recognizing the meanings in what they read (D) are all specific aspects of processing print structures used by proficient readers.

83. B: Proficient readers formulate hypotheses, incorporate ideas into larger constructs, and generate conclusions as they read. They also employ a variety of strategies to achieve comprehension of what they read rather than just one strategy (A). While proficient readers may love to read, one of their various strategies is also to understand the reason for reading a particular text, which is needed (C) to provide them with a focus when reading it. Another strategy used by students who read well is to reread or skim passages they have already read to increase their comprehension of them; they do not avoid this to prevent slowing their reading progress (D).

84. D: Providing students with many opportunities to read encourages reading proficiency by allowing them more reading practice. Providing the students with choices of reading materials (A) has also been shown to enhance their motivation to read because they have more control and choice than they do when reading only teacher-chosen materials, and because they can choose to read something that is personally appealing to them. When teachers can show students what is meaningful in what they read, students are more interested in reading (B). Teachers can also enhance students' motivation to read by making the activity fun (C).

85. D: Ms. Ross is presenting new words in multiple exposures to enhance vocabulary acquisition. Appropriate word choice (A) entails selecting words that are best suited to the particular instruction. Teaching word analysis (B) entails identifying word roots, prefixes, and suffixes, which greatly facilitates figuring out the meanings of new words. Contextual analysis (C) involves figuring out the meanings of new words by the context in which they occur.

86. D: In this example, Mr. Law is teaching his students word analysis by showing them how to break a complex word down into its prefixes, root words, and suffixes. Knowing these facilitates deducing the meaning of a word by knowing the meanings of each or some of the word's parts. Multiple exposures (A) would involve his presenting this same word to the class in repeated instances and a variety of contexts. Choosing appropriate words (B) would involve his making deliberate word choices that are congruent with his subject and level of instruction. Making a contextual analysis (C) would involve his asking the students to deduce the meaning of a word by finding clues in the sentence and/or the paragraph surrounding it.

87. B: Graphic organizers depict ideas and information in a variety of ways, and all of them are visual (e.g., charts, maps, pictures, etc.). These can be very helpful to students with disabilities who have trouble comprehending abstract concepts and/or organizing information because they make the material more concrete by using another modality. Teaching students how to summarize (A) helps them identify the important points or themes in reading material, and teaching them how to analyze the structure of a story (D) aids reading comprehension while employing critical thinking. Both of these skills will not directly make information visual unless they are taught specifically using graphic organizers (which include semantic organizers/maps). Using multiple strategies (C) is always highly recommended, but such strategies may involve a range of modalities, not simply a visual one.

88. A: Visual imagery is visual but not graphic, consisting of mental images that proficient readers form as they read, which can be taught through guided visualization. Graphic organizers are visual

126

and graphic, such as physical pictures (on paper, chalkboard or computer screens) rather than mental images. Venn diagrams (B) help to visualize comparisons and contrasts, using overlapping ovals or circles and placing shared features in overlaps. Concept maps (C) use boxes, circles, or other shapes containing words for concepts with lines or arrows drawn between them to indicate relationships or connections. Flow charts (D) aid in guiding decision-making and correctly sequencing the steps of an activity as well as showing hierarchical and organizational structures. Boxes are arranged and connected showing chronological order or positions in a hierarchy, and branches based on yes/no questions show alternative next steps.

89. A: The teacher's explication of the poem made its concept accessible to this student, who found it meaningful once he understood it. From his response, he found the message more meaningful than entertaining (B). While providing students with choices (C) and enough opportunities to read (D) are also teaching strategies that enhance reading proficiency, neither one was mentioned in this particular example. The teacher chose the short poem and it was an example of only one small opportunity to read.

90. B: This student has learned to perform the skills at home, but has not generalized them to other settings. It is superfluous to re-teach him the skills (A) because he has demonstrated their acquisition at home. Teaching skill maintenance (C) is unnecessary as the parents report he has performed the skills for years, so he has achieved maintenance but not generalization. Teaching skill discrimination (D) does not apply to this example as there was no mention of the student having any problems separating one skill or skill set from another or applying skills to the wrong tasks.

91. C: There are programs using student-directed curricula to promote self-advocacy. For example, Project LEAD (Pocock et al, 2002) is designed to empower students with disabilities by increasing their self-awareness about their disabilities and about academics and has been found effective. Federal legislation does specifically address self-determination (A): The Rehabilitation Act of 1997 states, "Disability is a natural part of the human experience and in no way diminishes the rights of individuals to live independently, enjoy self-determination, make choices, contribute to society...and enjoy full inclusion and integration into...the...mainstream of American society" (Sec. 1.2(a) (3)). Students with disabilities do not simply attain these skills at later ages than others (B); research finds they do not develop them without explicit instruction (Ellis et al, 1991). Student-led IEP conferences have been shown to benefit self-advocacy in disabled students (D): Lancaster, Schumaker, and Deschler's Interactive Hypermedia Program (2002) includes these and was found effective.

92. D: Self-advocacy training programs typically include instruction keeping track of their own progress and self-evaluating. For example, the Next S.T.E.P. curriculum (Zhang, 2001) teaches these skills. Self-awareness is a foundation and prerequisite for self-determination as well as social skills (A). Zhang (2001) found that the Next S.T.E.P. program significantly increased self-awareness for students with disabilities. Managing one's own transition plans is not a minor part of self-advocacy (B) but a major part. Indeed, the Next S.T.E.P. program is designed for making transitions between junior high and high school or high school and college. According to educational researchers, "The terminal goal for self-advocacy is to enable both general and special education students to have the opportunity for a smoother transition into post-secondary education and into the work force" (Pierson et al, 2005). The ability to set goals is not a prerequisite to participating in such programs (C), but is a skill they teach.

93. C: One component of explicit instruction required for students with high-incidence disabilities is the need to provide them with immediate feedback on their progress in developing self-advocacy.

As they will also need training in self-evaluation, they will not know how they are doing without this feedback. In addition to correction, they need feedback for positive reinforcement to continue. Other components include instructing them in the potential future value of the skills they are learning, not just in the skills themselves (A); providing them with opportunities not only to practice the skills taught, but also to observe them (B); and instruction in generalizing the skills being taught to real-world settings. Teaching rather than just doing is needed for generalization by these students (D).

94. B: Career orientation, also called career awareness, is the first stage of career development and should be initiated as early as possible so that young children develop self-confidence and self-worth. This helps them develop self-perceptions as workers, awareness of a variety of jobs, work values, and attitudes that are commensurate with their individual needs and strengths. Career exploration (A) is the second stage, which educators recommend initiating in junior high school. The first two stages also have lifelong applications. Career preparation (C) is the third stage and usually takes place when a student is a senior in high school. The final stage, career placement (D), initially culminates in job acquisition, but also includes follow-up and continuing education as an individual's needs, interests, goals, and priorities change over time.

95. A: With students who have disabilities, the time to introduce each career development stage depends more on the individual student's developmental level, which often is not commensurate with the student's grade level (B) or chronological age (D) in some or all domains. While the student's experiential level (C) is important for selecting instructional materials and methods, the developmental level has more impact on whether a student will be able to learn the skills acquired in each stage.

96. D: Some gifted students excel in all areas, including athletics and social skills (A), but not necessarily. Gifted children can have different abilities and interests than peers, making social interaction awkward. They may have difficulty relating to peers with more typical abilities and interests, resulting in peers who may not want to interact with them for being different. Some gifted children prefer academic/creative activities over social activities. Some gifted children show superior academic performance (B), while some do not. Some are bored by traditional curricula (including special education for the gifted) and lack motivation, while some use unconventional methods. As a child, Albert Einstein reportedly was failed in math by a teacher for achieving correct answers without following prescribed steps. Not all gifted children get high IQ scores (C) because giftedness also includes creativity, not just intelligence. Some gifted children do not respond to standardized measures because they may think differently and/or be uninterested in test items.

97. B: Career exploration, the second stage of career development, is usually a focus during junior high or middle school, although this may vary for students with disabilities by developmental level. Students learn about various occupational fields, about their own abilities and interests, and which occupations best fit them. They should be given opportunities for hands-on experiences in this stage. Career awareness (A) is the first stage, when younger children become aware of various jobs and develop values and self-concepts suited to future work. Career preparation (C) is usually in high school. Students define aptitudes and interests, choose courses, and develop skills and knowledge more specifically related to certain careers. Career placement (D) includes getting a job plus follow-up, continuing education, community agencies, guidance, and counseling services.

98. C: A student with disabilities may need support with transportation and assistive technology in order to live in the community as independently as possible and participate in community activities. County social workers, personal care providers, and others may attend to help in the personal and social (A) domain. Day habilitation and employment agency staff and vocational trainers may assist in the employment and career (B) domain. A staff member from the local Parks and Recreation Department could attend to provide transition services in the domain of leisure and recreation (D).

99. D: The 1997 version of IDEA required transition planning to begin when the student was 14 years old (C). The 2004 reauthorization of this law changed the age to 16. Some students with disabilities, such as those with autism spectrum disorders, often need extended time periods for transition planning, so many special educators still advocate beginning at age 14. Some individual states also specify age 14. The later age in the current reauthorization may reflect considerations related to developmental levels. Some students with disabilities need more time to complete secondary education. However, others will graduate at age 18 (A), so this can be too late for transition planning. (Legal rights to transition planning and services transfer from parents to students when the students turn 18.) Students with disabilities have the legal right to attend school until they graduate or reach the age of 22 (B), so transition planning must start before this.

100. A: Depending on the location, WorkAbility programs and Transition Partnership Programs (TPPs) may be integrated, or two separate but related programs. These programs are designed to connect the school's students with the community agencies and services they need. They are interagency programs formed in collaboration by state departments of education and/or of rehabilitation, county departments/offices of education, special education departments, school districts, etc. They also offer career counseling, job coaching, and job placement in addition to vocational education. Regional occupational programs (B), state conservation corps (C), and the Job Corps (D) (as well as community colleges and adult education programs) are all local vocational centers providing training in hundreds of different jobs. They are not specifically designed in cooperation with the schools.

How to Overcome Test Anxiety

Just the thought of taking a test is enough to make most people a little nervous. A test is an important event that can have a long-term impact on your future, so it's important to take it seriously and it's natural to feel anxious about performing well. But just because anxiety is normal, that doesn't mean that it's helpful in test taking, or that you should simply accept it as part of your life. Anxiety can have a variety of effects. These effects can be mild, like making you feel slightly nervous, or severe, like blocking your ability to focus or remember even a simple detail.

If you experience test anxiety—whether severe or mild—it's important to know how to beat it. To discover this, first you need to understand what causes test anxiety.

Causes of Test Anxiety

While we often think of anxiety as an uncontrollable emotional state, it can actually be caused by simple, practical things. One of the most common causes of test anxiety is that a person does not feel adequately prepared for their test. This feeling can be the result of many different issues such as poor study habits or lack of organization, but the most common culprit is time management. Starting to study too late, failing to organize your study time to cover all of the material, or being distracted while you study will mean that you're not well prepared for the test. This may lead to cramming the night before, which will cause you to be physically and mentally exhausted for the test. Poor time management also contributes to feelings of stress, fear, and hopelessness as you realize you are not well prepared but don't know what to do about it.

Other times, test anxiety is not related to your preparation for the test but comes from unresolved fear. This may be a past failure on a test, or poor performance on tests in general. It may come from comparing yourself to others who seem to be performing better or from the stress of living up to expectations. Anxiety may be driven by fears of the future—how failure on this test would affect your educational and career goals. These fears are often completely irrational, but they can still negatively impact your test performance.

> **Review Video:** <u>3 Reasons You Have Test Anxiety</u>
> Visit mometrix.com/academy and enter code: 428468

Elements of Test Anxiety

As mentioned earlier, test anxiety is considered to be an emotional state, but it has physical and mental components as well. Sometimes you may not even realize that you are suffering from test anxiety until you notice the physical symptoms. These can include trembling hands, rapid heartbeat, sweating, nausea, and tense muscles. Extreme anxiety may lead to fainting or vomiting. Obviously, any of these symptoms can have a negative impact on testing. It is important to recognize them as soon as they begin to occur so that you can address the problem before it damages your performance.

> **Review Video: 3 Ways to Tell You Have Test Anxiety**
> Visit mometrix.com/academy and enter code: 927847

The mental components of test anxiety include trouble focusing and inability to remember learned information. During a test, your mind is on high alert, which can help you recall information and stay focused for an extended period of time. However, anxiety interferes with your mind's natural processes, causing you to blank out, even on the questions you know well. The strain of testing during anxiety makes it difficult to stay focused, especially on a test that may take several hours. Extreme anxiety can take a huge mental toll, making it difficult not only to recall test information but even to understand the test questions or pull your thoughts together.

> **Review Video: How Test Anxiety Affects Memory**
> Visit mometrix.com/academy and enter code: 609003

Effects of Test Anxiety

Test anxiety is like a disease—if left untreated, it will get progressively worse. Anxiety leads to poor performance, and this reinforces the feelings of fear and failure, which in turn lead to poor performances on subsequent tests. It can grow from a mild nervousness to a crippling condition. If allowed to progress, test anxiety can have a big impact on your schooling, and consequently on your future.

Test anxiety can spread to other parts of your life. Anxiety on tests can become anxiety in any stressful situation, and blanking on a test can turn into panicking in a job situation. But fortunately, you don't have to let anxiety rule your testing and determine your grades. There are a number of relatively simple steps you can take to move past anxiety and function normally on a test and in the rest of life.

> **Review Video: How Test Anxiety Impacts Your Grades**
> Visit mometrix.com/academy and enter code: 939819

Physical Steps for Beating Test Anxiety

While test anxiety is a serious problem, the good news is that it can be overcome. It doesn't have to control your ability to think and remember information. While it may take time, you can begin taking steps today to beat anxiety.

Just as your first hint that you may be struggling with anxiety comes from the physical symptoms, the first step to treating it is also physical. Rest is crucial for having a clear, strong mind. If you are tired, it is much easier to give in to anxiety. But if you establish good sleep habits, your body and mind will be ready to perform optimally, without the strain of exhaustion. Additionally, sleeping well helps you to retain information better, so you're more likely to recall the answers when you see the test questions.

Getting good sleep means more than going to bed on time. It's important to allow your brain time to relax. Take study breaks from time to time so it doesn't get overworked, and don't study right before bed. Take time to rest your mind before trying to rest your body, or you may find it difficult to fall asleep.

> **Review Video: The Importance of Sleep for Your Brain**
> Visit mometrix.com/academy and enter code: 319338

Along with sleep, other aspects of physical health are important in preparing for a test. Good nutrition is vital for good brain function. Sugary foods and drinks may give a burst of energy but this burst is followed by a crash, both physically and emotionally. Instead, fuel your body with protein and vitamin-rich foods.

Also, drink plenty of water. Dehydration can lead to headaches and exhaustion, especially if your brain is already under stress from the rigors of the test. Particularly if your test is a long one, drink water during the breaks. And if possible, take an energy-boosting snack to eat between sections.

> **Review Video: How Diet Can Affect your Mood**
> Visit mometrix.com/academy and enter code: 624317

Along with sleep and diet, a third important part of physical health is exercise. Maintaining a steady workout schedule is helpful, but even taking 5-minute study breaks to walk can help get your blood pumping faster and clear your head. Exercise also releases endorphins, which contribute to a positive feeling and can help combat test anxiety.

When you nurture your physical health, you are also contributing to your mental health. If your body is healthy, your mind is much more likely to be healthy as well. So take time to rest, nourish your body with healthy food and water, and get moving as much as possible. Taking these physical steps will make you stronger and more able to take the mental steps necessary to overcome test anxiety.

> **Review Video: How to Stay Healthy and Prevent Test Anxiety**
> Visit mometrix.com/academy and enter code: 877894

Mental Steps for Beating Test Anxiety

Working on the mental side of test anxiety can be more challenging, but as with the physical side, there are clear steps you can take to overcome it. As mentioned earlier, test anxiety often stems from lack of preparation, so the obvious solution is to prepare for the test. Effective studying may be the most important weapon you have for beating test anxiety, but you can and should employ several other mental tools to combat fear.

First, boost your confidence by reminding yourself of past success—tests or projects that you aced. If you're putting as much effort into preparing for this test as you did for those, there's no reason you should expect to fail here. Work hard to prepare; then trust your preparation.

Second, surround yourself with encouraging people. It can be helpful to find a study group, but be sure that the people you're around will encourage a positive attitude. If you spend time with others who are anxious or cynical, this will only contribute to your own anxiety. Look for others who are motivated to study hard from a desire to succeed, not from a fear of failure.

Third, reward yourself. A test is physically and mentally tiring, even without anxiety, and it can be helpful to have something to look forward to. Plan an activity following the test, regardless of the outcome, such as going to a movie or getting ice cream.

When you are taking the test, if you find yourself beginning to feel anxious, remind yourself that you know the material. Visualize successfully completing the test. Then take a few deep, relaxing breaths and return to it. Work through the questions carefully but with confidence, knowing that you are capable of succeeding.

Developing a healthy mental approach to test taking will also aid in other areas of life. Test anxiety affects more than just the actual test—it can be damaging to your mental health and even contribute to depression. It's important to beat test anxiety before it becomes a problem for more than testing.

> **Review Video: Test Anxiety and Depression**
> Visit mometrix.com/academy and enter code: 904704

Study Strategy

Being prepared for the test is necessary to combat anxiety, but what does being prepared look like? You may study for hours on end and still not feel prepared. What you need is a strategy for test prep. The next few pages outline our recommended steps to help you plan out and conquer the challenge of preparation.

Step 1: Scope Out the Test

Learn everything you can about the format (multiple choice, essay, etc.) and what will be on the test. Gather any study materials, course outlines, or sample exams that may be available. Not only will this help you to prepare, but knowing what to expect can help to alleviate test anxiety.

Step 2: Map Out the Material

Look through the textbook or study guide and make note of how many chapters or sections it has. Then divide these over the time you have. For example, if a book has 15 chapters and you have five days to study, you need to cover three chapters each day. Even better, if you have the time, leave an extra day at the end for overall review after you have gone through the material in depth.

If time is limited, you may need to prioritize the material. Look through it and make note of which sections you think you already have a good grasp on, and which need review. While you are studying, skim quickly through the familiar sections and take more time on the challenging parts. Write out your plan so you don't get lost as you go. Having a written plan also helps you feel more in control of the study, so anxiety is less likely to arise from feeling overwhelmed at the amount to cover.

Step 3: Gather Your Tools

Decide what study method works best for you. Do you prefer to highlight in the book as you study and then go back over the highlighted portions? Or do you type out notes of the important information? Or is it helpful to make flashcards that you can carry with you? Assemble the pens, index cards, highlighters, post-it notes, and any other materials you may need so you won't be distracted by getting up to find things while you study.

If you're having a hard time retaining the information or organizing your notes, experiment with different methods. For example, try color-coding by subject with colored pens, highlighters, or post-it notes. If you learn better by hearing, try recording yourself reading your notes so you can listen while in the car, working out, or simply sitting at your desk. Ask a friend to quiz you from your flashcards, or try teaching someone the material to solidify it in your mind.

Step 4: Create Your Environment

It's important to avoid distractions while you study. This includes both the obvious distractions like visitors and the subtle distractions like an uncomfortable chair (or a too-comfortable couch that makes you want to fall asleep). Set up the best study environment possible: good lighting and a comfortable work area. If background music helps you focus, you may want to turn it on, but otherwise keep the room quiet. If you are using a computer to take notes, be sure you don't have any other windows open, especially applications like social media, games, or anything else that could distract you. Silence your phone and turn off notifications. Be sure to keep water close by so you stay hydrated while you study (but avoid unhealthy drinks and snacks).

Also, take into account the best time of day to study. Are you freshest first thing in the morning? Try to set aside some time then to work through the material. Is your mind clearer in the afternoon or evening? Schedule your study session then. Another method is to study at the same time of day that you will take the test, so that your brain gets used to working on the material at that time and will be ready to focus at test time.

Step 5: Study!

Once you have done all the study preparation, it's time to settle into the actual studying. Sit down, take a few moments to settle your mind so you can focus, and begin to follow your study plan. Don't give in to distractions or let yourself procrastinate. This is your time to prepare so you'll be ready to fearlessly approach the test. Make the most of the time and stay focused.

Of course, you don't want to burn out. If you study too long you may find that you're not retaining the information very well. Take regular study breaks. For example, taking five minutes out of every hour to walk briskly, breathing deeply and swinging your arms, can help your mind stay fresh.

As you get to the end of each chapter or section, it's a good idea to do a quick review. Remind yourself of what you learned and work on any difficult parts. When you feel that you've mastered the material, move on to the next part. At the end of your study session, briefly skim through your notes again.

But while review is helpful, cramming last minute is NOT. If at all possible, work ahead so that you won't need to fit all your study into the last day. Cramming overloads your brain with more information than it can process and retain, and your tired mind may struggle to recall even previously learned information when it is overwhelmed with last-minute study. Also, the urgent nature of cramming and the stress placed on your brain contribute to anxiety. You'll be more likely to go to the test feeling unprepared and having trouble thinking clearly.

So don't cram, and don't stay up late before the test, even just to review your notes at a leisurely pace. Your brain needs rest more than it needs to go over the information again. In fact, plan to finish your studies by noon or early afternoon the day before the test. Give your brain the rest of the day to relax or focus on other things, and get a good night's sleep. Then you will be fresh for the test and better able to recall what you've studied.

Step 6: Take a practice test

Many courses offer sample tests, either online or in the study materials. This is an excellent resource to check whether you have mastered the material, as well as to prepare for the test format and environment.

Check the test format ahead of time: the number of questions, the type (multiple choice, free response, etc.), and the time limit. Then create a plan for working through them. For example, if you have 30 minutes to take a 60-question test, your limit is 30 seconds per question. Spend less time on the questions you know well so that you can take more time on the difficult ones.

If you have time to take several practice tests, take the first one open book, with no time limit. Work through the questions at your own pace and make sure you fully understand them. Gradually work up to taking a test under test conditions: sit at a desk with all study materials put away and set a timer. Pace yourself to make sure you finish the test with time to spare and go back to check your answers if you have time.

After each test, check your answers. On the questions you missed, be sure you understand why you missed them. Did you misread the question (tests can use tricky wording)? Did you forget the information? Or was it something you hadn't learned? Go back and study any shaky areas that the practice tests reveal.

Taking these tests not only helps with your grade, but also aids in combating test anxiety. If you're already used to the test conditions, you're less likely to worry about it, and working through tests until you're scoring well gives you a confidence boost. Go through the practice tests until you feel comfortable, and then you can go into the test knowing that you're ready for it.

Test Tips

On test day, you should be confident, knowing that you've prepared well and are ready to answer the questions. But aside from preparation, there are several test day strategies you can employ to maximize your performance.

First, as stated before, get a good night's sleep the night before the test (and for several nights before that, if possible). Go into the test with a fresh, alert mind rather than staying up late to study.

Try not to change too much about your normal routine on the day of the test. It's important to eat a nutritious breakfast, but if you normally don't eat breakfast at all, consider eating just a protein bar. If you're a coffee drinker, go ahead and have your normal coffee. Just make sure you time it so that the caffeine doesn't wear off right in the middle of your test. Avoid sugary beverages, and drink enough water to stay hydrated but not so much that you need a restroom break 10 minutes into the test. If your test isn't first thing in the morning, consider going for a walk or doing a light workout before the test to get your blood flowing.

Allow yourself enough time to get ready, and leave for the test with plenty of time to spare so you won't have the anxiety of scrambling to arrive in time. Another reason to be early is to select a good seat. It's helpful to sit away from doors and windows, which can be distracting. Find a good seat, get out your supplies, and settle your mind before the test begins.

When the test begins, start by going over the instructions carefully, even if you already know what to expect. Make sure you avoid any careless mistakes by following the directions.

Then begin working through the questions, pacing yourself as you've practiced. If you're not sure on an answer, don't spend too much time on it, and don't let it shake your confidence. Either skip it and come back later, or eliminate as many wrong answers as possible and guess among the remaining ones. Don't dwell on these questions as you continue—put them out of your mind and focus on what lies ahead.

Be sure to read all of the answer choices, even if you're sure the first one is the right answer. Sometimes you'll find a better one if you keep reading. But don't second-guess yourself if you do immediately know the answer. Your gut instinct is usually right. Don't let test anxiety rob you of the information you know.

If you have time at the end of the test (and if the test format allows), go back and review your answers. Be cautious about changing any, since your first instinct tends to be correct, but make sure you didn't misread any of the questions or accidentally mark the wrong answer choice. Look over any you skipped and make an educated guess.

At the end, leave the test feeling confident. You've done your best, so don't waste time worrying about your performance or wishing you could change anything. Instead, celebrate the successful completion of this test. And finally, use this test to learn how to deal with anxiety even better next time.

> **Review Video: 5 Tips to Beat Test Anxiety**
> Visit mometrix.com/academy and enter code: 570656

Important Qualification

Not all anxiety is created equal. If your test anxiety is causing major issues in your life beyond the classroom or testing center, or if you are experiencing troubling physical symptoms related to your anxiety, it may be a sign of a serious physiological or psychological condition. If this sounds like your situation, we strongly encourage you to seek professional help.

Thank You

We at Mometrix would like to extend our heartfelt thanks to you, our friend and patron, for allowing us to play a part in your journey. It is a privilege to serve people from all walks of life who are unified in their commitment to building the best future they can for themselves.

The preparation you devote to these important testing milestones may be the most valuable educational opportunity you have for making a real difference in your life. We encourage you to put your heart into it—that feeling of succeeding, overcoming, and yes, conquering will be well worth the hours you've invested.

We want to hear your story, your struggles and your successes, and if you see any opportunities for us to improve our materials so we can help others even more effectively in the future, please share that with us as well. **The team at Mometrix would be absolutely thrilled to hear from you!** So please, send us an email (support@mometrix.com) and let's stay in touch.

If you'd like some additional help, check out these other resources we offer for your exam:

http://MometrixFlashcards.com/FTCE